ALL THAT'S GOOD

The story of **Butch Stewart**, the man behind **Sandals Resorts**

Sandow Media Corporation

BOCA RATON, FLORIDA

ALL THAT'S GOOD

The story of **Butch Stewart**, the man behind **Sandals Resorts**

Pamela Lerner Jaccarino

Foreword by **Sir Richard Branson**

Sandow Media Corporation
Boca Raton, Florida

Produced and published by Sandow Media Corporation, Inc.
©2005 All rights reserved. No portion of this book may be reproduced—mechanically, electronically, or by any other means, including photo-copying—without written permission from the publisher, except for brief passages that may be quoted for reviews.

Library of Congress Catalog Card Number 2004195505

ISBN: 0-9764713-0-2

First Printing May 2005

10 9 8 7 6 5 4 3 2 1

Printed in China

CEO AND PUBLISHER	Adam I. Sandow
CREATIVE DIRECTOR	Yolanda E. Yoh
MANAGING EDITOR	Pamela Lerner Jaccarino
SPONSORSHIP DIRECTOR	Linda G. Frank
PRODUCTION MANAGER	Jody Scalla
PRODUCTION ARTIST	Andrew Kemp
COPY EDITOR	H. Susan Mann

Sandow Media Corporation is a cutting-edge publishing company built around a single philosophy: always exceeding expectations. Based in Boca Raton, Florida, Sandow Media Corporation is defined by an unrelenting drive toward quality and innovation. Founded in 2001 by Adam I. Sandow, Sandow Media specializes in developing consumer books and magazines in the categories of travel, shelter and beauty. Sandow Media builds uniquely positioned publications that thrive both in print and online. Creativity is at the core of every segment of its business and is evident in all its products and brands.

SANDOW|MEDIA™
Always Exceeding Expectations

CORPORATE HEADQUARTERS
3731 FLORIDA ATLANTIC UNIVERSITY BOULEVARD
BOCA RATON, FLORIDA 33431
TELEPHONE 561.750.0151 FAX 561.750.0152
WEB www.sandowmedia.com

PRESIDENT AND CHIEF EXECUTIVE OFFICER Adam I. Sandow
CHIEF OPERATIONS AND FINANCIAL OFFICER Scott R. Yablon
CORPORATE EDITORIAL AND CREATIVE DIRECTOR Yolanda E. Yoh
EXECUTIVE VICE PRESIDENT Erik I. Herz
GROUP PUBLISHER Michael J. Ruskin
VICE PRESIDENT OF OPERATIONS Lloyd Gilick
MANAGING EDITOR Pamela Lerner Jaccarino
GROUP PUBLISHER (LUXE™ PUBLICATIONS) Dana L. Meacham
REGIONAL PUBLISHER Linda G. Frank
ADMINISTRATION Shirley M. Costa, Eric Fields, Maritza Severino
GENERAL COUNSEL Boies, Schiller and Flexner; Michael Kosnitzky, Esq., Keith Blum, Esq.

TABLE OF CONTENTS

ACKNOWLEDGMENTS

Countless individuals contributed to the making of this book, from longtime and original team members with Appliance Traders Limited and Sandals to former employees, travel industry executives and government officials. I would like to thank the dozens of folks—housekeepers, general managers, taxi drivers, waiters, and corporate executives—who sat down with me to recount their stories.

Much credit goes to Mandy Chomat, for initiating this project; to John Lynch, Maggie Rivera, Tony Cortizas, and the Unique Vacations public relations and advertising team, for all their efforts; to David Roper, for his wise counsel and unwavering support throughout this project; to Jaime Stewart and other Stewart family members, for their insight and for rummaging through old photo albums; to Betty Jo Desnoes, for her information on the early years and for lending me a treasure trove of albums filled with newspaper clippings; and to Arlene Lindo, for all of her kind assistance. Special thanks also goes to Melbourne Alexander, Barrington Bennett and Charles Lumpkin, for putting up with my insistence that they forklift down dozens of old cobweb-covered boxes tucked away on the highest shelves of the twenty-foot-high corporate warehouse so I could hunt for archive photographs. The effort was well worth it.

Certainly, this book would not be possible without Adam Sandow, who brought his incredible vision and leadership to the project, and Linda Frank, who spearheaded our sponsorships with her impeccable professionalism and enthusiasm. And, of course, we thank our many sponsors for their tremendous support.

Finally, thanks to Butch Stewart for one helluva story.

Pamela Lerner Jacccarino

THE PUBLISHER WOULD GRATEFULLY LIKE TO ACKNOWLEDGE OUR SPONSORS, WHO MADE THE PUBLISHING OF THIS BOOK POSSIBLE

PLATINUM

Air Jamaica
Air Jamaica Vacations

American Airlines Vacations
GOGO Worldwide Vacations

Pevonia Botanica Skincare
Travel Impressions, Ltd.

GOLD

Air Canada Vacations
Appleton Jamaica Rum
The Burns House Group
of Companies
Cable & Wireless Jamaica Ltd.

Colombian Emeralds International
Condé Nast Bridal Group
Departures Magazine/
Travel + Leisure Magazine
Jamaica Broilers Group Limited

JUTA Tours Ltd.
Life of Jamaica Limited/
Sagicor Financial Group
The Mark Travel Corporation
Ty, Ty, & Ty, Inc.

SILVER

Arosa Ltd.
Associated Manufacturers
Bank of Saint Lucia Ltd.
Blue Mountain Bicycle Tours
Bridal Guide Magazine
Classic Custom Vacations
Dunn's River Falls and Park
Ferguson Enterprises
Garber Travel

Green Grotto Caves and
Attractions
Go Classy Tours, Inc.
Happy Vacations
IE Limited
Implementation Ltd.
Jamaica Tourist Board
Margaritaville
Patti LaBella Travel

Pleasant Holidays
Rapsody Cruises
RBTT Financial Holdings Limited
Signature Vacations
The Knot
Travelweek
Trip Mate Insurance Agency, Inc.
WeddingChannel.com

BRONZE

Adler Insurance Group
Agostini Insurance Brokers
(St. Lucia) Limited
Aqua Sun Video & Photos
A Time to Travel
Cairsea Services
Carisam-Samuel Meisel
Chukka Adventure Tours Ltd.
Citibank, Jamaica
Cool Runnings Spring Water Co, Ltd.
Edward Don & Company

Expedia.com
Harris Paints (St. Lucia) Ltd.
Heave-Ho Charters
Islands Media
JAG Incorporated
Jamaica Money Market Brokers Ltd.
Larry Kline Wholesale Meats
Mair Russell Grant Thorton
Majestic Tours
MasterCraft International Sales
MLT Vacations Inc.

Nassau Paradise Island
Promotion Board
PricewaterhouseCoopers
Protection & Security Ltd.
Renwick & Company Ltd.
St. Lucia Tourist Board
Sant Associates Architect
The Shell Company (W.I.) Limited
Tortuga Rum Company Ltd.
Travel Agent Magazine
Travelocity.com

PATRONS

Anderson Fabrics, Inc.
ART Sound Lighting & Video
Brinks St. Lucia Ltd.
Captain Mike's Sport Fishing &
Pleasure Cruises
Caribbean Communications Network
(CCN)
Caribbean Metals Limited
Carnival Party Cruises
Far Eastern Imports
Flight Centre North America

Guardian Holdings Limited
Guardsman Limited
Hill & Hill
J.A. Prime Gourmet Foods Inc.
Jack Tobin Inc.
Jamaica Tours Ltd.
Jay Stelzer & Associates
Julian's Supermarkets
Lou Hammond & Associates, Inc.
Martha Stewart Living Omnimedia

McNamara & Co.
New York Magazine
P/Kaufmann Contract
St. Lucia Distillers
Steelite International
& Inter-brand Inc.
Tourisme Plus
TravelAge West
Travel Weekly
Video Ventures Limited

COMMITTED TO EXCELLENCE

You've got to love a guy who knows how to build a brand, especially a maverick like Butch Stewart! He's got guts, determination and one of the most fascinating stories in the travel business. Butch is the type of an entrepreneur that I truly respect. He started out humbly, selling air conditioners, and went on to create a successful appliance trading company based on the motto "committed to excellence." Next, Butch took a risk by venturing into tourism, an industry he knew nothing about. Yet he had a vision, remained steadfast to his ideals, and blazed a trail, building one of the travel industry's most globally recognized brands.

I've been delighted to work with Butch Stewart. We're proud to work together promoting the Caribbean, one of the world's most stunning regions.

Like Virgin, Sandals is committed to improving the customer's experience in innovative ways. And, likewise, the company is part of a family, with shared values and a dedication to the communities it serves, always reaching higher, always getting better.

Sir Richard Branson
May 2005

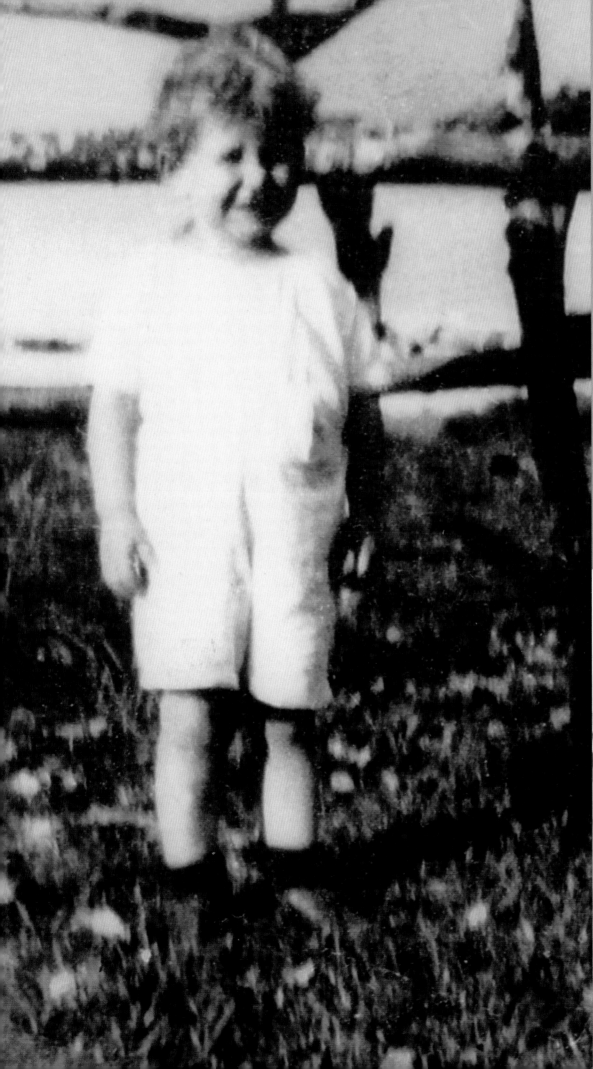

Stewart's lineage has deep Jamaican roots. Opposite: His great-great grandfather, Herbert Edward Coxe, far left, was, at the time, Custos of St. Ann, Jamaica. He is pictured along with Stewart's great grandfather, James Ernest La Courdaire Coxe and Stewart's grandfather, James Rupert Stewart Coxe, at Ramble Estate, their farm in St. Ann, circa 1896. The family grew tea, along with other crops. This page: Left: Gordon Leslie Stewart, Butch Stewart's father in his youth. Below: His mother, Jean Stewart and father, Gordon Leslie Stewart.

1 The Trader King

I THINK THAT WE WILL NEVER SEE
A BUSINESSMAN AS BOLD AS HE;
A MAN WHOSE AIM IS EVER HIGH,
WHOSE ONLY LIMIT IS THE SKY.

APPLIANCES HAVE WON HIM FAME,
BUT HOTELS ARE ALSO HIS GAME; AT
HOME, IN BOARDROOM OR ON BEACH,
COMMANDING EVERYTHING IN REACH.

IN THESE DAYS OF STRESS AND
STRAIN, HE RECORDS NOT LOSS BUT
GAIN; SUCCESS IS THE SONG I SING:
HERE'S TO BUTCH, THE TRADER KING!

From a cartoon in the *Jamaica Gleaner*

Even with cool trade winds blowing into St. Mary, on Jamaica,

summers were apt to be quite warm.

This year, Mr. Clive Duncan, a successful young businessman living in the parish, intended to do something about it. Though it was considered a luxury to have a home air conditioner in 1969, Duncan wanted to surprise his wife with one for her upcoming birthday.

But work got the best of him. The gift slipped his mind until the night before his wife's special day. Now he was really in a bind. He recalled hearing about a man who ran a small air-conditioning business in Kingston and could do quick installations. Duncan called Appliance Traders Limited the next morning and spoke with owner Butch Stewart. "Fedders is the best air-conditioning brand in the world," Stewart boasted. And, he advised Duncan that ATL could install the unit within eight hours. Duncan considered the prospect for a moment: He could give his wife the surprise gift tonight, on her birthday. He had only to arrange for them to be away from home all day, and the housekeeper would let the installers in. When they returned in the evening, the house would be cool; he had Stewart's guarantee.

That said, the deal was done. Butch Stewart and his team, including ace technician Errol Lee, had to move fast. It was already eleven o'clock and their destination, St. Mary, was two hours away.

"We loaded the unit and the tools into the back of Mr. Stewart's Mercedes-Benz and took off," recalls Errol Lee, one of Stewart's first employees, now ATL technical quality-control manager. "When we reached the home, the place was locked up and we could not find the housekeeper, or anybody. We knew we were in trouble. Our reputation was based on delivering a certain level of service and getting the units installed on time. I remember Mr. Stewart saying, 'There's just no way we've come down here to turn and go back with that unit.' So, we resorted to desperate measures. We broke into the house and did what we had to do. The unit was installed as planned and we left the home in tip-top shape."

Another satisfied customer for the Trader King!

LIVING CAREFREE

Gordon Arthur Stewart, known as "Butch," was born in Kingston on July 6, 1941. His professional, working-class parents, Jean and Gordon Leslie Stewart, raised Butch on Jamaica's north coast, in Ocho Rios, just a small coastal town back then. "Growing up in that kind of environment, where everybody looks out for everybody in the community is very healthy. It doesn't come better than that," Stewart recalls fondly.

Stewart lived by the sea in a home named *Aguazul,* part of the property now known as Sandals Grande Ocho Rios Beach & Villa Resort. Full of energy, the north coast way of life suited Stewart's happy-go-lucky disposition. He enjoyed a carefree Huck Finn type of childhood: fishing, swimming and sailing. He prized these much more than, say, attending school. "I grew up by the sea," says Stewart. "It was always a struggle not running away to go fishing or skin diving rather than going to school."

Classrooms, lesson plans and homework were not his thing and he dropped out of school at age 14. Shortly thereafter, Stewart concocted his first foray into tourism.

Recalls childhood neighbor and past ATL general manager Mike Sharpe: "As young teenagers, Butch and my older brother had a little twelve-foot boat built for themselves, mostly for fishing and stuff. But Butch figured a way he could turn that boat into a small business. Even then, he always worked harder than everybody else. There was a young fellow in the village, a very nice, jovial guy who everybody knew. Well, Butch convinced

the nickname

"My son was a very big baby, weighing nine and a half pounds at birth," recalled Gordon L. Stewart, Butch's late father, who was affectionately known as Daddy Stew. "Little Gordon was loveable, with a rough-and-tumble nature to him. He reminded us of this playful bulldog called Butch on a popular cartoon at the time. So we decided to call him Butch and it has stuck with him ever since."

him to take the boat up to Plantation Inn, a resort just up the coast, and get tourists to pay for boat rides. The venture worked for a little while, that is until the boat sank. You see, they were so eager for the boat that regular plywood instead of marine ply was used!"

A few years later, Stewart traveled to England to finish his education. Before long, he returned to Jamaica and became a salesman for the Dutch-owned Curacao Trading Company. In six years, he learned the business and worked his way up to the position of sales manager. But the entrepreneurial spirit called. Stewart wanted to work for himself. At the age of 27 he ventured out on his own.

"Even then, he always worked harder than everybody else."

BALANCING ACT
As a young man, Stewart balanced working hard at odd jobs with the pleasures of taking off for a day on the open seas or other adventures.

SOMETHING IN THE AIR

In the late 1960s on Jamaica, having an air conditioner in your home was a luxury. "It was like buying a Cadillac for your wife," says Stewart. "An air conditioner in a master bedroom at that time was a big investment."

Envisioning a business opportunity for himself, a determined Stewart pounded the pavement, knocking on doors in Kingston and selling in-room window air conditioners. With a natural flair for sales, he soon succeeded in his goal of writing thirty orders. There was just one hitch: He didn't have a single air-conditioning unit to install. Unfazed, Stewart sent a letter to Fedders, an air conditioner manufacturer based in New Jersey, asking the company to grant him a distributorship for the island. But without an established company or

BREAKING GROUND
Soon regarded as a cutting-edge company, Appliance Traders Limited was headquartered in Kingston and added a branch office in Ocho Rios, pictured at right, in 1972.

> A determined Stewart pounded the pavement, knocking on doors in Kingston and selling in-room window air conditioners.

big-time funding, he was having difficulty getting a response.

Resolute to get what he wanted, Stewart flew to New Jersey and met with several executives, giving them his pitch. It was an effort to close the sale, though, until he met the president's nephew, Bruno Giordana. Stewart made a compelling presentation, the two hit it off, and Giordana authorized the deal. Finally, Stewart had the break he needed.

With his savings of $3,200 and plenty of moxie, the young man from St. Ann opened Appliance Traders Limited on June 1, 1968, at 15 Caledonia Avenue, in the Cross Roads area of Kingston. His first small team—O.G. Green, Taddy Fletcher, Irving Broderick, "Gussy" Thomas, Bunny Griffiths, David Grant, Errol Lee, and Check Nicholas—helped with installation and service, while Stewart's first wife, Erica, handled administrative matters.

From the outset, Stewart desired to be number one.

"We had a little old building that we fixed up as best we could. When the funds couldn't stretch any further, we settled for a plywood door with four rough legs for my desk," recalls Stewart. "It was the best desk I ever had, so spacious nothing fell off it!"

In the beginning, ATL was the underdog in Jamaica's burgeoning air conditioner market, competing with name brands like Carrier, York, General Electric and Westinghouse. But from the outset, Stewart desired to be number one, the best. He was clever enough to realize that ATL needed a niche in addition to hard work and resolve—something that no one else had. Stewart came up with a unique concept: speedy installations.

"We were the only company that was able to offer an eight-hour installation job anywhere in Jamaica," recalls Errol Lee. "When anyone purchased an air conditioner from ATL, we would have it installed and working within eight hours. So, if you ordered an air conditioner in the morning, by the time you came back from work you had a nice, cool home."

"We were number one within the year," says Stewart.

●MEET ERROL LEE
FACTORY MANAGER

FINDING A NICHE
According to Errol Lee, Stewart made a decision to emphasize customer satisfaction and build a reputation for reliability, particularly in after-sales service.

satisfaction

"Mr. Stewart built his business based on the belief of giving the customer immediate gratification. As soon as he got a call from a customer and put the phone down, he wanted us to be on the spot within ten minutes to make an impression on the customer. So enthusiastic were we to please that customer that one day I wrote off three motor vehicles. Yes, three accidents in one day, just trying to get from point A to point B to satisfy those customers!"

ERROL LEE
TECHNICAL QUALITY-CONTROL MANAGER
APPLIANCE TRADERS LIMITED

One Love

Jamaica's aura is irresistible. So it's not surprising that the island's tourism developed rapidly and has become its leading industry. Jamaica dazzles with the jewel colors of tropical blooms. Grand mountains and cerulean seas dominate the landscape. Jamaica is the land of "one love," basking beneath the sun that perpetually shines upon its spirited people.

The island's rich heritage is a true melting pot of world cultures. The resulting vibrancy, color, creativity, and flair are reflected in every aspect of life, from language to cuisine to rare personalities. It is a national characteristic to break through boundaries in a constant quest to be the best.

In its role as destination marketers, the Jamaica Tourist Board partners with the industry's hoteliers, tour operators and airlines to offer an enriching travel experience.

"The ability to cater wondrously to a diversity of tastes has been nowhere better demonstrated in the Jamaican hotel sector than in the Sandals resorts," says Paul Pennicook, Jamaica's tourism director. "The resorts exude an Old World charm while the staff delivers first-world professional service. Certainly, the chain has been an outstanding and integral part of the development of Jamaica's tourism product."

"Butch has stood like a colossus in Jamaica's tourism," Pennicook continues. "He is a true visionary, demanding and innovative, with an uncanny eye for the details which elevate the superior to the sublime. The Jamaica Tourist Board applauds Sandals as a driving force in the island's tourism industry and commends its role in inspiring Jamaica to even greater heights."

Photos: Jamaica Tourist Board

FAMOUS VISITOR: A highlight of Appliance Traders activities during 1981 was the visit in September of Joseph P. Kennedy II (at left), who toured the company'splant in Kingston while in Jamaica. Here he is seen in discussion with Larry McDonald, a Director of ATL (centre), and Michael Fuller, refrigeration technician. His visit to Jamaica was in connection with ATL's installation of solar equipment at the Cornwall Regional Hospital in Montego Bay.

The pursuit of excellence in quality and service was at the core of Butch Stewart and his first company, Appliance Traders Limited. "Committed to Excellence" remains the company motto. He expects it of himself and demands it of his workforce. "He only ever sold the best product and gave the best service," says Stewart's longtime executive assistant and right hand, Betty Jo Desnoes. "He never compromised. He knew everything that was going on and was very fastidious in all that he did and all that was done."

Stewart made sure that his company ideals were passed down to each and every employee. "Butch instilled in us the philosophy that a good, quality sales department could only sustain itself by having the best, most efficient service," says Errol Lee. "And that has stuck with me to this day."

Longtime ATL employee and now group director of engineering for Sandals Resorts International Larry McDonald concurs, "One of the things that struck me about Butch was that his service meetings would go on until seven, eight, nine o'clock at night. He hammered home the point that service must be the key to everything you do and that you must let people know that the brand names ATL represents are the best."

A KENNEDY CONNECTION
Joseph P. Kennedy, far left, tours the Appliance Traders plant in 1981 on a visit to Jamaica. Kennedy and Stewart hit it off and became lifelong friends.

Jamaica Money Market Brokers

Vision of Love

In 1992, Jamaican phenomenon Joan Duncan, known as JD, a single mother of five children, started her first company, Jamaica Money Market Brokers Limited (JMMB).

Her vision for the company was to make the money market available to all Jamaicans. Together with Dr. Noel Lyon, JMMB's current chairman, her dream became a reality. JD sought to develop a company based on the values of love, integrity and mutual respect. By 1995, JMMB was established as a major player in the Jamaican financial sector and the firm was regarded as one of Jamaica's most dynamic, innovative and efficient financial institutions.

JMMB continues to subscribe to her vision.

When JD died in 1998, her dream had been fulfilled. JMMB had a capital base of J$190 million and over twenty thousand accounts. Today, under the direction of JD's older children, Donna and Keith, JMMB is the leading financial brokerage house in Jamaica.

"THE PHILOSOPHY WAS TO GIVE MORE THAN WAS EXPECTED IN TERMS OF SALES. THE TECHNICIANS WERE TRAINED SO THAT WHEN THEY HAD FINISHED WITH THE INSTALLATION OF THE AIR CONDITIONER, THEY ASKED THE HOUSEWIFE, 'DO YOU HAVE ANY OTHER NEEDS? CAN I LOOK AT YOUR FRIDGE? CAN I LOOK AT YOUR STOVE? DO YOU NEED A BULB CHANGED?' THEY ALWAYS WENT BEYOND THE EXPECTATION. REGARDLESS OF WHAT SOMEONE PAID FOR, YOU WERE TO GIVE THEM EXTRA."

Eleanor Miller
Former ATL Branch Manager,
now Director of Projects
for Sandals Resorts International

"I grew up by the sea."

— Gordon "Butch" Stewart

SWEET FLEET
Ace technicians at Appliance Traders Limited pose next to their spotless vehicles. Every truck and car was painted with the blue Fedders logo.

Soon enough, Kingstonians were abuzz about Appliance Traders and the Fedders brand name, thanks in part to Stewart's ingenious way of spreading the word. In those days, Stewart drove a white 1968 Mercedes-Benz 250. The car was a beauty and a sight to behold. Stewart kept it immaculate. Yet it possessed an unusual characteristic, particularly for a pricey Benz. A large letter "F" was painted in the Fedders logo style on both passenger doors. It showed that Stewart was not only proud of his business but also a great marketer. The logo car was a hit. And, as Appliance Traders Limited grew and acquired service vehicles, mostly Volkswagen vans, the company immediately painted the ATL logo, blue Fedders logo and other name brands the company represented on them. "For the first time in Jamaica, we had mobile billboards," boasts McDonald. Affectionately known as "The Blue Birds," the ATL flock of vehicles was the talk of the town.

Stewart was not only proud of his business but also knew how to market it.

"Nobody in their right mind thought about displaying Fedders, or anything else for that matter, on a Mercedes-Benz," recalls Eleanor Miller, former ATL branch manager and now director of projects for Sandals Resorts International. "Everybody in Jamaica thought he was mad, and they certainly talked about it! The vehicles proved to be big advertising tools. The ATL fleet had the cleanest, prettiest vehicles, and they had all this writing all over them. In those days, it was unheard of. Nobody was doing anything like that then. And by doing things like that he grew Fedders into the largest brand of air conditioners in Jamaica."

Dunn's River Falls and Green Grotto Caves

Along Jamaica's sun-drenched, sea-washed legendary north coast lies the garden parish of St. Ann, home to two principal natural treasures—Dunn's River Falls and Park, and Green Grotto Caves and Attractions.

Dunn's River Falls, just a stone's throw from the resort town of Ocho Rios, has the distinction of being the only waterfall of its kind in the Caribbean, if not the world, that beckons visitors to come climb it.

Yes, you are allowed to climb these falls in a human chain led by experienced Falls guides. Those less brave may view the activities of the more adventuresome from the secure vantage point of the terrace or deck.

The Falls reveals a delightful new discovery around every turn. Those who enjoy Mother Nature's gifts can lose themselves in lush tropical foliage. Souvenir hunters can browse through the shops in the craft park. Or, they can commission their own piece, climb the falls and collect it on their return.

Over at Discovery Bay is famous Green Grotto Caves, the first caves worldwide to have received the Green Globe certification for high environmental standards. The labyrinthine limestone cave with its numerous rock formations is the focus of this natural attraction.

Green Grotto Caves is rich in history. The first Jamaicans, known as the Arawak Indians, or Tainos, once sought shelter in these caves. When the English were taking over the island, the caves were used as a hideout for Spaniards who were being driven out of the country. They were also used by smugglers running arms to Cuba in the mid-1920s. During the Second World War, the Government of Jamaica used the entrance of one of the caves as a storeroom for barrels of rum.

Within eighteen months of operation, the company purchased land at No. 7 Marescaux Road in Cross Roads and built the first ATL building. Thanks to Stewart and his dedicated team, Fedders now controlled 53 percent of the residential air-conditioning market and was breaking into the commercial sector. Continued rapid growth and a demand for service in the resort areas led to a decision to expand to Jamaica's north coast. Larry McDonald was hired as manager to handle the expansion and launch the new Ocho Rios branch.

McDonald recalls fondly: "I arrived at the ATL head office at Marescaux Road. After waiting a short time, I was greeted by Butch with his trademark charismatic 'Hi, baby!' I looked around and, not seeing any babies, assumed he was addressing me. We walked into his office and he stated that opening the Ocho Rios branch was 'no big deal.' He quickly rattled off a to-do list: Remove the current renter of the site, which was a lime factory; knock down the building; hire an architect to design a new building; oversee the construction; put together a workforce; and start earning some money! 'You've got three months.'"

Five months later, on May 17, 1972, Appliance Traders Limited opened a branch office on Newlin Street in Ocho Rios. "The Blue Birds" spread their wings over Jamaica's north coast.

BUTCH'S BOYS
Opposite: Stewart's late son, Jonathan, at left, and son Bobby, at right, who is today managing director for Sandals Resorts International in the United Kingdom, proudly sit atop their dad's Benz. Left: The ATL show-room and office located at 35 Halfway Tree Road in Kingston.

Mair Russell Grant Thornton

Managing Business

Founded more than twenty years ago, Grant Thornton has a long track record of helping companies as they expand and explore business internationally. This leading financial and business adviser to independent owner-managers and their businesses has more than 585 offices in 110 countries and provides accountancy, tax and business advice. Grant Thornton focuses on the owner-managed and entrepreneurial business sectors and continues to develop services and products tailor-made to them.

The firm of Mair Russell Grant Thornton represents Grant Thornton locally on Jamaica. The company prides itself on valuing performance as the key to its success. Mair Russell has forged long-term relationships with its clients, including Sandals, which have endured economic and market uncertainties.

"Our clients have grown to rely on our corporate strategy designed to ensure a superior level of service, locally and globally," says Kenneth L. Lewis, senior partner, Mair Russell Grant Thornton.

Photo: Sandals Resorts International

Living Carefree

In 1840, The Barbados Mutual Life Assurance Society established itself as an indigenous provider of mutual insurance for the island of Barbados. Through the years, the company expanded its offices and diversified its business into banking and other financial services. Even as it grew, the company maintained its regional approach to providing insurance and financial services.

In 2002, the company demutualized and was renamed the Sagicor Financial Group. With the acquisition of Life of Barbados and Life of Jamaica, Sagicor consolidated its position in the sector and is now the island's primary provider of life and health insurance, mortgages, and pension and administrative services. The name "Sagicor" comes from the word "sage" and was chosen to reflect the organization's new vision for financial advice and services.

Dodridge D. Miller
President

Commenting on the name change, Sagicor's president and chief executive officer, Dodridge Miller, says, "Our new name and identity draw on the strength, stability and financial prudence that are our heritage. And this identity also represents the freedom that wise financial thinking can bring to our customers throughout their lives."

Today, Sagicor Financial Group provides a comprehensive range of financial solutions to its customers and is uniquely positioned as the leading home-grown Caribbean financial services institution, one that understands the needs and shares the aspirations of all the people of the region. As a diverse regional group, it employs over fifteen hundred people and operates twenty-two offices in twenty countries across the Caribbean, Latin America and the United States.

Leaders in Life

Any history of Life of Jamaica must return to the point where the mantle of British rule was thrown off and Jamaica stood forth as a free nation. Independence, on August 6, 1962, brought a sense of urgency, purpose and challenge. The spirit of nationalism was everywhere, especially in political, economic and cultural spheres. The 1960s saw a Jamaican Miss World, Marcus Garvey as Jamaica's first national hero, the establishment of Air Jamaica as the country's airline, and a number of breakthroughs in business, education and the arts. The process of change, led by the government of Sir Alexander Bustamante, was under way.

Across the country, people felt the urge to develop new projects, to explore new ideas, to accomplish new missions. Propelled by this energy, six enterprising Jamaicans, namely Danny Williams, Adrian Foreman, Manley McAdam, Donald Davidson, Herbert Hall, and Peter Rousseau, spearheaded a project to establish the first Jamaican-owned life insurance company.

Maxine MacLure
President and CEO

Armed with the self-confidence inherent in their outstanding professional track records acquired from working for North American Life Assurance Company of Canada (NALACO), the group began negotiations, which culminated with the formation of Life of Jamaica.

On the new venture's first day of operations, with a field force of sixty-five insurance agents, the company wrote more than one million dollars in life insurance. The company also achieved the distinction of being the first insurance company to be listed on the Jamaican Stock Exchange.

Today, Life of Jamaica Limited, a member of the Sagicor Financial Corporation, is the leading life insurance company in Jamaica, and has a solid reputation as a pacesetter, innovator and leader in the Caribbean life insurance industry.

Even as the company expanded, Stewart remained the center of ATL. He made it his business to know everything that was going on with every customer and was on a first-name basis with his staff. He knew what they did and how they did it. Not only did they work for him, he considered them and treated them as friends. "We worked hard, but had a ball. Everyone felt that way," recalls Miller. "There was little division between work and play."

Yet behind Stewart's easygoing, informal personality was a get-down-to-business attitude where work ethics and standards were anything but casual. "His standards were always very, very high," says Miller. "I remember when he'd stand around back and watch the technicians drive up in their pickups. He'd stop them and say, 'Let me see this engine.' If you couldn't 'eat off of the engine,' there was a problem. The uniforms they wore had to be immaculate and wearing jeans, for example, was unacceptable. The cars had to be clean. The showroom had to be spotless. Everything had to be meticulous."

WORK AND PLAY
Opposite: Loyal staff gather awaiting the arrival of their boss, Butch Stewart, to celebrate his birthday
Right: All ATL vehicles were equipped with two-way radios for rapid response.

ON 24-HOUR CALL: Senior service technician, Bunny Griffiths, checking in with base, from his radio-controlled service vehicle. All Appliance Traders vehicles are equipped with two-way radio, which allows the service team to respond to calls at a moment's notice.

Citibank Jamaica

Financial Well-Being

Peter Moses
Citigroup Country Officer

Citibank Jamaica's meaningful and mutually beneficial relationship with Sandals Resorts began some thirty years ago. As a young entrepreneur, Butch Stewart met Bill Rhodes, a young banker from the United States who was on assignment in Jamaica with Citibank N.A., then known as First National City Bank. At the time, Stewart convinced Rhodes to grant him a loan to further develop his appliance business.

Since then, Stewart and Rhodes have grown to be established leaders in their respective fields. Stewart has become a tourism and airline industry icon while Rhodes became an international banker and one of the most senior officers of Citigroup, the world's largest financial institution.

"Butch Stewart is an inspiration for young Jamaicans who want to make it in business," says Peter Moses, Citigroup's country officer. "He has shown that with hard work and a commitment to service, the sky's the limit."

In 1975, Appliance Traders Limited branched out into the automotive business with the acquisition of Caribbean Brake Products Limited, a company that was originally established in 1959. Caribrake, as it is known locally, manufactures a complete range of automotive brakes, clutches and filter products for Japanese, European, American and British vehicles. Caribrake was one of the first companies in Jamaica to recycle and it is highly regarded for its prominent role in the country's recycling program.

Below: Stewart, far left, and the Caribrake team take time out to kick a few rims.

MARKETING MASTER

ATL continually improved its service by being innovative, particularly in the area of sales and marketing. Stewart was a salesman who could "sell ice to the Eskimos" and he was a brilliant marketer who understood the importance of promoting his products. Even with a commodity like air conditioners, Stewart somehow always found ways to put his own creative mark on whatever he sold.

"I remember the second week that I joined the company," recalls McDonald. "One Friday, Butch called us all together and told us that we were going to load up the ATL vans with every product that we sold and have a motorcade all through the affluent neighborhoods. Sure enough, the next day, on Saturday, at 11 a.m., the parade

"He motivated us all by the way he went about conducting his business."

took off. All of our painted-up Volkswagen vans were loaded with every appliance and brand. Someone had a microphone and talked up the products and the company over the microphone. We were all there, including Butch. And we actually got quite a number of folks to come out."

Profits were invested back into the company to ensure a greater level of service to the customer. For example, ATL was one of the first Jamaican companies to use mobile radio-controlled units for greater speed and efficiency. As the company purchased additional vehicles, it equipped them with two-way radios, establishing contact with the base station for greater efficiency.

"Early on, everyone had radios and there was constant communication," remembers McDonald. "You called back to the base to report on your work status. To Mr. Stewart, keeping in touch and communication was key. Service personnel had to call in every fifteen minutes, reporting their location, job progress and availability for new jobs."

GETTING DOWN TO WORK

What is Butch Stewart's secret? This young man with an easy, down-to-earth Jamaican charm set seemingly impossible high standards, demanding that his employees meet the mark. And they did every time. Where did he get this knack for being able to harness the full potential of each and every one of his employees? Why did they drive themselves so hard, pushing themselves through fifteen-, eighteen-hour days, working all crazy hours of the night?

"He motivated all of us by the way he went about conducting his business," reflects Lee, "and he never asked you to do anything that he himself would not do. He came to the office at seven o'clock in the morning every day, although the office opened at eight o'clock."

Desnoes recalls: "He worked as hard as anybody else. He was part of the team and was not just giving instruction and going home at five o'clock."

That tenacity would come in handy in the early 1970s as Jamaica's landscape and business climate were altered by then Prime Minister Michael Manley. Taxes were levied on luxury goods like air conditioners and the government mandated that businesses limit imports and turn to manufacturing. The consequences for Appliance Traders were severe.

THE TRADER KING
Right: Stewart made a name for himself with ATL and he was featured, in 1985, in a cartoon entitled "Trader King" by Leandro, which appeared in the *Jamaica Gleaner*.

Not one for dawdling, Butch Stewart did what had to be done. It was time to take action: ATL changed with the times and expanded into manufacturing, producing household appliances, air conditioners, water pumps, electrical generators and other items. Within the year, all goods were being manufactured and ATL dominated the air conditioner market.

In September 1973, ATL moved to its present location at 35 Halfway Tree Road in Kingston. The company had grown from residential air conditioner sales to manufacturing and to representing the top appliance brands—Amana refrigerators and freezers, Sunroc watercoolers, Panasonic fans, and KitchenAid dishwashers and a host of others.

Life was good. Butch Stewart and his outstanding team had achieved much and were a success. But the government then stipulated that foreign exchange for imports was limited to foreign exchange earners. Stewart needed a vehicle through which he could earn foreign exchange. Tourism seemed to be the ticket.

TRADER KING

I think that we will never see
A businessman as bold as he:
A man whose aim is ever high,
Whose only limit is the sky.

Appliances have won him fame,
But hotels also are his game:
At home in boardroom or on beach
Commanding everything in reach.

In these days of stress and strain
He records not loss, but gain:
Success is the song I sing,
Here's to Butch, the Trader King!

Gleaner Annual, December 1985

The team at American Airlines Vacations believes that a vacation should be as individual as the customer purchasing it.

Ready for

American Airlines provides its customers with more choices.

Take-off

In March 1971, Caribbean tourism got a big boost when American Airlines gained its first Caribbean routes through a merger with Trans Caribbean Airways. American inaugurated service by flying between New York and five Caribbean destinations—Puerto Rico, Aruba, Curaçao, the U.S. Virgin Islands, and Haiti. The airline expanded those routes throughout the early '70s and acquired other Caribbean routes in 1975 from Pan American World Airways.

Today, American and its regional affiliate, American Eagle, depart from more than thirteen North American cities to more than thirty-six destinations in the Caribbean, and to the Bahamas and Bermuda in the Atlantic.

The team at American Airlines Vacations believes that a vacation should be as individual as the client purchasing it. To that end, the company offers customers the opportunity to customize vacations by offering an expansive network of flights, hundreds of hotels across all price ranges, numerous options for rental cars or other transportation, and a host of activities and features from which to choose. All-inclusive vacations have proved to be very popular with its clients.

American's impressive fleet transports guests to the Caribbean

"For more than ten years now, American Airlines Vacations, a leader in the vacation travel industry, has offered Sandals resorts in our extensive Caribbean product line," says Dan Westbrook, president of American Airlines Vacations. "Butch Stewart and his team are innovators and leaders in the industry, and we've formed a terrific working partnership over the years. We are proud to be associated with Sandals Resorts, and we especially value the tremendous job they do of taking care of our customers, who always seem to come home happy."

Getting to Sandals and Beaches resorts with American Airlines Vacations is easy. The tour operator features the quality of American Airlines service in the air and is backed by American Airlines on the ground. What's more, the airline has a long-standing and well-known dedication to the region.

For more than thirty years, American Airlines has worked closely with governments, hoteliers and tourism authorities to promote travel and tourism in the Caribbean and in the Bahamas and Bermuda.

In 1992, American, in conjunction with government and private-sector leaders, helped develop a regional marketing campaign. This effort established the Caribbean Coalition for Tourism—a partnership of government officials, Caribbean Hotel Association representatives and other private-sector partners—who sell and market the region for tourism.

"Butch Stewart and his team are innovators and leaders in the industry."

DAN WESTBROOK
PRESIDENT

American's goal is to maximize the quality of its service to all its destinations in the Caribbean.

American has steadily upgraded and expanded its facilities throughout the Caribbean, and it has invested heavily in the airport in Miami and in San Juan, Puerto Rico, its two hub cities serving the Caribbean. At Luis Muñoz Marín Airport in San Juan, American has remodeled and expanded its terminal facilities at a cost of $300 million, including ticket counters, gate areas, the Admirals Club, and baggage areas. There also are new Customs and Immigration facilities. In Miami, a $1.7 billion expansion is planned.

American Airlines is grateful for the support that it has received from travel agents, governments, hoteliers, its passengers, and its employees in the region. American's goal is to maximize the quality of its service to all its destinations in the Caribbean.

American Eagle, American's regional partner, has also expanded its facilities in San Juan. Eagle invested $6 million in a gate facility that can handle as many as fifteen flights simultaneously and has seating capacity for three hundred passengers.

American Airlines Vacations, a division of American Airlines, is one of the most recognized airline-owned tour operators. With more than fifty years of experience, American Airlines

Vacations offers its customers comprehensive, cost-competitive tour packages to more than fifteen hundred hotels and resorts in more than three hundred worldwide destinations, including California, Canada, the Caribbean, Florida, Europe, Hawaii, Las Vegas/Reno, and Mexico.

2

Brave
New Venture

MR. STEWART DID NOT BRING A
TRADITIONAL HOTELIER'S APPROACH
TO RUNNING A RESORT. HE TAUGHT
ME, AND MANY OTHERS, THAT IF THE
GUEST WANTS SOMETHING, FIND A
WAY TO GIVE IT TO THEM.

David Roper
Group Director, Industry Relations
Sandals Resorts International

In its heyday during the 1950s, the Bay Roc Hotel had a

sterling reputation and was considered one of Jamaica's most venerable hotels. Back in the glamour days of travel, well-heeled couples journeyed to Jamaica, enjoying the comfort of exclusive hotels and private cottages. They soaked up the sun by day and, at twilight, donned elegant attire for an evening of cocktails and smart conversation.

"I thought, why would he be investing his money in this half-dead hotel."

By the mid-1970s, lifestyles changed and so did the pace of travel. Jamaica's tourism had suffered under Prime Minister Michael Manley's socialist government, and it was not the best time to be in the hotel business. International hotel chains and investors with capital fled the island en masse. Bay Roc hotel had deteriorated and owner Dick DeLisser was looking to sell.

The 1980 elections brought the Jamaican Labour Party into power, and it seemed as if the tourism climate might turn for the better. Still, times were sketchy and few private investors were willing to dip their toes back into the tourism pool.

It was during this rough patch, when everyone was pulling out, that Butch Stewart—with no hotel experience—plunged in. He purchased the Bay Roc hotel and Carlyle on the Bay from DeLisser in April 1981. Both properties were located in Montego Bay, Jamaica's most popular tourist area.

Commenting on Stewart's new venture, Anthony Abrahams, former minister of tourism for Jamaica, said: "I thought he was crazy. Despite whatever faith he might have had in the new government coming in— and I was minister of tourism at that time, charged with reconstructing the tourist industry—I thought, 'why would he be investing his money in this half-dead hotel.' I had been a tourism technician all my life and believed he was ill-advised to buy Bay Roc."

PRIME PROPERTY
Nearly all tourism officials thought Stewart took a risk when he purchased Bay Roc, above, and Carlyle on the Bay, left, though early staffers were pleased with the venture.

SANDALS

A BRAVE NEW VENTURE

story on Page 2

Most everyone agreed. The resort was in bad shape. While others saw a run-to-the-ground hotel situated next to the runway of Montego Bay's airport, Stewart focused on the property's strong points. The resort had sixty-six spacious hotel rooms in its Almonds block and thirty privately owned cottages, which were marketed by the hotel. Best of all, Bay Roc sat on a magnificent stretch of shoreline, which happens to be one of the island's largest private beaches.

Yes, the resort may have had cracked pipes and shoddy wiring, but that could all be worked on. What was critical now was finding the consummate hotel operations man to run the still-open-for-business, fifty-two-room Carlyle on the Bay and to assist in establishing Bay

SERVICE WITH A SMILE
Whether attending to rooms or serving beverages beachside, Sandals hotel staff is trained to cater to guests.

Roc. Stewart turned to friend Tony Hart, who set up a casual meeting with another acquaintance, a man named Merrick Fray.

"When I first met Butch Stewart I remember thinking, 'well, he's much younger than I expected,'" recalls Fray, the first Sandals employee, who later became managing director for Sandals Resorts International. "As the general manager of Seawind Hotel, I had dealt with Appliance Traders. I knew it as a good company that gave me great service. So, we had a little chat and he explained that he was looking to purchase the two hotels and that he was looking for a general manager. I felt strongly that I had something to offer him, and I indicated that if he wanted someone to handle running both hotels, I was his man. Then he asked me a question, which kind of stumped me, 'What do you know about marketing?' And I said, 'Absolutely nothing!' I remember him kind of sighing, 'Ohhh,' as if it wasn't what he wanted to hear. But little did I know that I was speaking to the marketing guru of all time. He said, 'Why don't you come to Kingston?' And I did.

"We really didn't know what we were buying, except that it had a fantastic beach."

"He showed me around Appliance Traders, I met some of the team players, and then, just like that, he said, 'Merrick, I want you to go to Montego Bay and take the keys to Carlyle.' And that was that. I sat in the general manager's seat and took over Carlyle on the Bay, which was operating as an European Plan hotel. I had a background as a controller, so I immediately set up all the accounting systems and generally was chief cook and bottle washer."

With the very first employee now hired, hotel operations were under way. But a few miles away, over at Bay Roc, the resort was far, very far, from being ready to accommodate guests.

"I don't think Mr. Stewart realized how bad the hotel was beneath the surface and how much work was ahead," says David Roper, who started with Sandals as a general manager and is now group director of industry relations for Sandals Resorts International. "Perhaps he thought all the hotel would need was a lick of paint." That certainly was not the case. In trademark fashion, Stewart used his wits and his resources. And so, with a roll-up-your-sleeves mentality, the Appliance Traders team was summoned to help work on the hotel's infrastructure. "We handled everything from electric to air-conditioning to plumbing," recalls Errol Lee.

Unwary staff were in for a few, shall we say, temporary lifestyle changes as well. One morning at the Appliance Traders office in Kingston, Stewart approached his employee Aston "Plum-Plum" James, a dedicated master plumber and jack-of-all-trades. He said, "Plum-Plum, come take a ride with me. We're going down to Montego Bay to look at something." Well, Plum-Plum didn't get back home for nine months; he had to send for his clothes. He remained in Montego Bay, basically running the first project office on-site, and was instrumental in getting the hotel up and running.

TEAM SPIRIT
Early members of the Sandals team still with the company today include Merrick Fray, second from right, and Karen Sprung, far right.

In trademark fashion, Stewart used his wits and his resources.

fish tales

Two leisure pursuits that just might entice Butch Stewart away from work—for a short time, at least—are dominoes and fishing. The boy who once fished from a canoe, today sports a 132-foot yacht called *Lady Sandals*, among other crafts. Deep-sea fishing off the coast of the Bahamas is a constant lure. Perhaps the attraction is a relaxing day at sea or the thrill of reeling in a big fish, which is particularly appealing to Stewart, who is always up for a challenge of any kind.

Opposite: Stewart, with former wife, P.J., shows off his catch of the day. Naturally, it's an impressive one.

Visitors choosing JUTA travel in comfort and style and also enjoy personalized service.

Tops in

Equipped with special training, JUTA drivers often double as impromptu tour guides.

When it comes to getting around Jamaica's 4,442 square miles, the Jamaica Union of Travellers Association Ltd., popularly known as JUTA Tours, gets visitors where they want to go.

Established in 1973, JUTA Tours operates as Jamaica's number one ground transportation operator for both the local and international tourism communities. Equipped with a modern fleet of well-maintained air-conditioned cars, buses, coaches, and luxury vehicles, each piloted by experienced and friendly drivers, JUTA is the choice for visitors looking for more than just a way to get from one place to another.

Transport

of the island's attractions, every JUTA driver is certified by the Jamaica Tourist Board, and as such has attended seminars about Jamaica's history, culture, geography, and flora and fauna. Equipped with this special training, JUTA drivers often double as impromptu tour guides. En route, they happily entertain passengers with interesting historical facts, bits of local trivia and rural lore.

JUTA Tours offers an array of island tours, taking visitors to Dunn's River Falls for climbing, to Negril for sunset watching, to the Martha Brae for river rafting, and to the island's great houses for a dose of island history.

Recognized by the Jamaica Tourist Board and The Jamaica Hotel and Tourist Association, JUTA Tours has enjoyed a long-standing involvement with Sandals. "We have always had the support of Butch Stewart, even at the initial stage of his involvement in tourism," says Garfield Williamson, JUTA president. "We take great pride in transporting Sandals guests and do so with professionalism, experience, responsibility, and efficiency, which we strive for in all our endeavors."

The JUTA Tours team consists of highly trained certified representatives, drivers and tour guides. "We are totally committed to going the extra mile for our customers," adds Williamson. "We are in the hospitality business and understand that, for many visitors, we are the first point of contact, greeting guests with a warm welcome. Making a great first impression and keeping it is vital for our industry."

Headquartered in Montego Bay, JUTA Tours expanded its presence over the years, and today boasts offices in Negril, Ocho Rios, Falmouth, Kingston, and Port Antonio. In addition to serving airports and seaports with ground transfers, JUTA Tours runs a thriving guided tour business, coordinates meetings and incentive group programs, and stages familiarization trips.

Choosing JUTA means that not only will visitors travel to their destination in comfort and style, but they will also enjoy personal service, all in all making for a memorable Jamaican experience. JUTA drivers have a reputation for being more than simply drivers—they are also regarded as being affable, dependable and knowledgeable about their island home. In other words, they are friendly and make excellent tour guides. Ready to shuttle guests to and from their destination, or to take them on a personalized tour

CRAFTING THE CONCEPT

Butch Stewart wanted to develop a striking new concept for the Carlyle property, which had been a traditional European Plan hotel. He sensed it wasn't going to work the way it was and recognized that he had to be as innovative as he had been in the early days of Appliance Traders Limited. How was he going to do this? He was an air-conditioning guy who didn't know anything about hotels or how the industry worked. "The advantage is that he's a born marketer," says Fray. "Mr. Stewart did a lot of background investigating and talked to hoteliers to find out: What does the industry want? What does the customer want?"

Stewart wanted to give customers what they desired and more—to exceed their expectations. So he broke with tradition and went with his gut, adding

"What does the industry want?

innovations that were unheard of at the time. "Butch Stewart pioneered what is now commonplace and set the standard by which all other hotels are measured," Fray continues. "King-size beds and clock radios were installed in every room, as were hair dryers. Guests could enjoy large, comfortable satellite-television lounges, and all other manner of little luxuries. He did this because he wanted his hotel to be different from the rest. Nobody put hair dryers in the rooms in those days! As far as the couples-only concept, well, at the time, statistics showed that 88 percent of Americans who traveled to the Caribbean traveled as male/female couples. So after the lovebirds we went and set about to create the finest, most romantic resort for two people in love."

Stewart admits, "At first we didn't know what to do with the property. So we took a long look at the all-inclusive, couples-only resorts. Then we kind of modified that concept, with more of an emphasis on luxury, though it was still pretty primitive by today's standards."

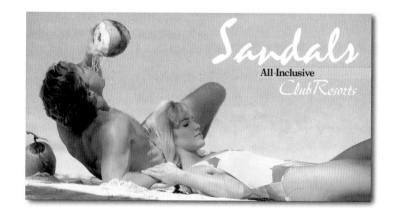

Sandals
All-Inclusive
Club Resorts

What does the customer want?"

With the winter season fast approaching, the group had to move quickly, which was never a problem for Stewart or his team. "It was get the decisions made and then action," recalls Betty Jo Desnoes, who along with P.J., Stewart's wife at the time, handled all of the interior design. "It was do this, do that, do the other, and make things come together as quickly and properly as possible."

Architect Evan Williams clearly recollects the timeline: "I got a call from Butch, who said he recently bought the properties and wanted me to meet with him. When I got to Bay Roc, he was sitting on this derelict reception counter. The place was a mess. He said he wanted to open it in sixteen weeks and that it was going to be a new all-inclusive. The activity was so intense during those four months. We slept at the site, and worked and slept in shifts. Plum-Plum, Mr. Stewart, myself, and Larry McDonald. That was an early indication of the success they would go on to have, and the hands-on approach."

Attitude, energy and eighteen-hour days were what it would take to renovate the site. Major repairs and refurbishments were under way to the tune of two million dollars. Natural Jamaican-pink Trelawny cut stone was brought in to make a dramatic new entrance. A solar-paneled skydome was erected some forty-eight feet above the parquet floor. New tropical foliage was planted everywhere.

welcome

"At Sandals, even the arrival process was an innovation. Champagne arrivals were very important so that when guests arrived there was a party feeling. We didn't want anybody to go up to a front desk and just register. They would come in, the music would start, and they would be offered champagne. Everyone was actively involved in receiving that first guest and those that followed. The process was key to setting the tone for the rest of their vacation. We would have the place humming with staff everywhere, balloons decorating the entrance and a band playing in the lobby. Cold towels and champagne greetings were totally unknown in the industry at the time, but for us it was the norm."

BALDWIN POWELL

GENERAL MANAGER

SANDALS REGENCY ST. LUCIA GOLF RESORT & SPA

Not only did a new lobby and pool have to be built, so did a team of resort staff members.

"Appliance Traders had made a good little name for itself in Jamaica because we'd do any level of somersault for people to ensure that they were happy," says Stewart. "If someone called at midnight and wanted an air conditioner because he'd forgotten to buy a birthday present for his wife, we'd go out and install it right away. We just transferred that attitude to the hotel business. Even though we didn't know anything about the resort business, there were a lot of people who did, so we put together a team."

Tony Henry, the first general manger of Bay Roc, along with then food and beverage manager Brian Roper and entertainment director Basil Cahusac, among others, helped start up and develop that team.

"From very early on, actually from the first day, we set a philosophy of employing the right people, whether they were front desk staff, Playmakers, managers, or water-sports staff," explains Brian Roper, who is now group director of operations for Sandals Resorts International.

"We were trained in everything from stagecraft and microphone techniques, to addressing guests and hosting shows."

One of those first bright young stars hailed from Canada. Karen Sprung, an original member of the Playmakers—a troupe of gregarious, talented hosts and hostesses who kept things moving on property 24/7— recalls the scene when she visited the property in late spring, 1981: "My friend Cheryl Atkinson picked me up from the airport and drove me to this dilapidated hotel where she was working. It looked like a war zone. The sky dome had no dome; it was just a big hole. The pool was just being built. We were walking up, down and around planks and boards. But there was energy and a certain vibe to the place. I accepted the job on the spot."

THAT'S ENTERTAINMENT
**Above: Consummate hotel entertainment director Basil Cahusac.
Far left: Sandals Playmakers climb high. Left: Bikini-clad entertainers.**

SHOWTIME
Playmakers, standing by the piano, rehearse the evening's entertainment.

"We started training in Cottage 1 and 2 under the direction of veteran resort entertainment director Basil Cahusac," recalls Sprung. "Myself, Rosy Phillips, Cheryl Atkinson, Diane Armstrong, Anna Kay Harrison, and Neal Tavares were the original Playmakers crew. What Basil taught us was probably some of the best background in entertainment and theater training anyone could have. We were instructed in everything from stagecraft and microphone techniques, to addressing guests and hosting shows. It was all done with complete professionalism. He gave us all the tools we needed in order to succeed."

Successful training was also taking place in Cottage 6. Here's where the distinguished, Old School-trained head maitre d', Robert Stone, was hiring and teaching the ropes to his dining-room staff. "When I started work, I brought over some of my waiters from Jack Tar Beach Village, where I had been working," says Stone. "I conducted service-training classes on how to set a table, how to serve guests, just overall dining-room service etiquette. Those were busy times. Contractors and builders were all around the place, but things didn't drag on. Mr. Stewart wanted things done fast."

Chukka Adventure Tours

Off We Go!

Every year, about seventeen thousand guests of Sandals and Beaches resorts on Jamaica seek adventure off-property. They find it riding horseback in the warm Caribbean Sea, tubing down a jungle river, and careening through the lush countryside in a Jeep or ATV safari.

For over eighteen years, Chukka Adventure Tours, now in Ocho Rios and Montego Bay, has been providing exhilarating, memory-making excursions for guests who want to explore Jamaica's dramatic scenery and have a dash of adventure. Exclusive adventures include an underwater walk to a coral reef and The Original Canopy Tour®, which enable participants to swing between high platforms in the trees while harnessed onto traverse cables.

"Like Sandals, we're a family business," says Chukka Cove founder and chairman, Danny Melville. "And we are proud to share Jamaica's natural beauty and exciting attractions."

" WHEN WE HIRE STAFF, WE LOOK FOR PEOPLE WITH A GOOD ATTITUDE. THIS IS A SERVICE INDUSTRY AND YOU MUST HAVE A SMILE. WHEN I INTERVIEW PEOPLE I SPEND A LOT OF TIME WITH THEM, GAINING AN INSIGHT INTO THEIR BACKGROUND AND THEIR LIFE. ONE KEY AREA I LOOK AT IS THE PERSON'S AMBITION. I WANT TO KNOW IF THEY HAVE A SENSE OF GROWTH AND IF THEY WANT TO GET SOMEWHERE. IF SOMEONE IS PROGRESSIVE AND SHOWS A DEGREE OF LEADERSHIP, THEN THEY WILL CATCH ON TO OUR VISION. "

Merrick Fray
Managing Director
Sandals Resorts International

"The unique manner in which we distill, hand blend and bottle our rums helps contribute to their inimitable quality."

JOY SPENCE
MASTER BLENDER

Get in the

Appleton is proud to be the official rum of Sandals and Beaches Resorts.

While Sandals was starting up what would eventually become one of Jamaica's best-loved getaways, another island legacy was toasting its rich heritage with a splash of its own. The history of Appleton Jamaica Rum dates back to 1749. At Jamaica's oldest sugar estate, situated in the Nassau Valley on both sides of the Black River in southwest Jamaica, estate owners got their first taste of a sure thing. Over two hundred and fifty years later on the same eleven thousand acres

Spirit

of rich soil known as the Appleton Estate, the world's finest rum is still being distilled. Produced only in Jamaica, Appleton Estate Rums may harken back to the days of the old plantations but are now enjoyed by everyone from near and afar.

While Cognac may brag of brandy and Scotland swanks single malts, Jamaica revels in its Appleton Rum. Both locals and visitors appreciate the delicious libation, still produced following the Estate's time-honored traditions. Master Blender Joy Spence, distinguished for being the first woman to achieve this position in the industry, oversees production.

"Our process is perfected at every step," says Spence. "From selecting our vast sugarcane varieties to the special yeast culture used in fermentation, everything is done meticulously."

When the Sandals team was seeking to stock a signature rum, they turned to Appleton. No wonder. The company is regarded for its range of award-winning blends—Appleton Special Jamaica Rum and Appleton Estate VX Jamaica Rum, being two favorites. The sweet libations proved so popular that Sandals took them one step further, of course, opening official Appleton bars at several Sandals properties. Vacationers stroll the grounds or sit on bar stools enjoying their rum cocktails. With so many blends to choose from, how do guests know which one to select?

Here's a guide to some of Appleton's premier rums.

Appleton Estate V/X Jamaica Rum, the flagship brand, is a full-bodied, medium sweet rum indicative of the famous estate rums for which Appleton is renowned. It's a smooth and mellow blend of rums that has been aged for up to ten years. Enjoy Appleton Estate V/X in cocktails such as Mai Tai's and rum martinis.

Appleton Estate Reserve Jamaica Rum is a super premium blend that has been aged for up to twelve years. This full-bodied aged rum masterpiece is so harmonious that the whole transcends the sum of its many parts.

The rums that make up Appleton Estate Extra have been aged for up to eighteen years. The long years of tropical aging give this blend its mahogany hue, bold character and smooth taste, which

Joy Spence
Master Blender for Appleton Rums

invites favorable comparison to the world's finest cognacs and scotches.

The luxury blend Appleton Estate 21 Year Old Jamaica Rum is a smooth sipping rum that will please the most discerning connoisseur. Made up of a blend of rums that have been aged for a minimum of twenty-one years, it can be enjoyed neat, on the rocks or with a splash of water.

Cheers!

Concrete was poured. Staff were schooled. Now the property had to be properly marketed. Once again, the Trader King was in need of a niche. Smart enough to ask for advice, Stewart turned to those in the know to handle the marketing details. Jean Jutan, a young hotel veteran who worked for Jamaica Resort Hotels in Miami and had successfully marketed many Jamaican resorts during the tough '70s, was brought on as vice president of sales and marketing.

"Butch contacted me soon after he acquired the properties," Jutan recalls. "At the time, there were a few all-inclusive resorts, like Couples, Trelawny Beach and Hedonism, which were doing well. Butch knew he wanted to have an all-inclusive property, and he also felt that specializing as a couples-only resort was the way to go. He would always say, 'When you want to be the best, specialize.'"

Jutan had to get cracking in order to promote Bay Roc and make sure it was included in tour operator brochures for the winter season. She needed to hire an advertising agency to come

"When you want to be the best, specialize."

up with a marketing piece that would drive the message home, which was that Bay Roc provided the very finest vacation for two people in love. Jutan rang up Adrian Robinson, a bright young Jamaican advertising executive working at an advertising agency in Orlando, Florida.

"I was working with a tourism marketing company by the name of Robinsons Inc., no relation," recalls Adrian Robinson, a former director of tourism for Jamaica. "Doing a tourism marketing plan for, let's say, Puerto Rico, Mexico, or anywhere else, was okay; but anytime there was an opportunity to work with a Jamaican hotel, the juices started pumping and we were really eager and geared up to do the work. We just got very excited about the whole thing. When I heard from Jean that Butch bought the properties, I said, 'Hey, let's talk about this.' He said, 'Fine, Let's see what you can come up with.'

SALES CALL
Right: Displaying Sandals' first marketing material, created by Adrian Robinson, a former director of tourism for Jamaica, Jean Jutan, left, hits the trade show circuit, promoting the new resort to tour operators.

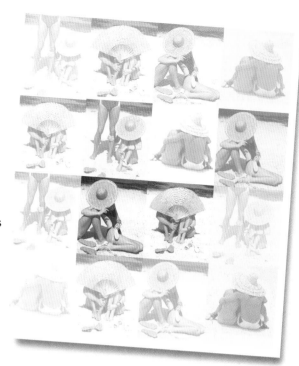

"At the time, it seemed that Butch had decided to call the hotel *Club Bay Roc*. I said to him that there's just no way you can call it that for all kinds of reasons. It's not a good marketing name. It's not a good brand to go to market with. *Bay Roc* doesn't mean anything I said.

Calling it *Club* was, in those days, the trend many hotels were taking when they wanted to go all-inclusive because they wanted to follow the Club Med idea. And that's exactly why I didn't want to go that route. Since Club Med had led the way, I knew anything named Club thereafter was going to be following as a 'me, too.' It seemed to me that there was an opportunity to establish something totally distinctive and different. *Club Bay Roc* just wasn't going to cut it. So I said, 'Let me think of something.' I sat down and started thinking about it, and I worked on it solid for a weekend. At about three o'clock on Sunday afternoon, it just came to me: *Sandals Resort Beach Hotel*. It was perfect for all kinds of reasons. It said relaxation. It said vacation. It said laid-back. And it created a graphic in your head that you could associate it with. In terms of brand awareness, it was just a much better way to go. However, the term *Club* did manage to sneak its way into the name."

MasterCraft

Show Boat

What's one of the most popular activities at Sandals and Beaches? Water sports. When Noylis Amair, Sandals Group director for water sports, was looking to upgrade the program in the early days, he turned to MasterCraft.

Vacationers at Sandals and Beaches can now brush up on their water-skiing skills or take their first fledgling attempts knowing they are behind one of the many MasterCraft world-class towboats. The MasterCraft ProStar 190 and ProStar 197 are the only towboats in the world certified in all five competitive water-sport events.

Founded in 1968, MasterCraft's team of designers developed a boat-industry innovation — a hull that yielded the smallest wake in the industry, a godsend for many. The crafts were highly regarded for being smooth and low at slalom and jump speeds and well defined at trick speeds. Today, MasterCraft is the market leader in inboard water-ski, wakeboard and luxury performance powerboats.

Secure with MasterCraft towing the line, Sandals' guests dive in for vacation fun.

"Forget about hotels and lead with hospitality."

On November 27, 1981, Sandals Resort Beach Club welcomed its first guests. "We all trekked over to the airport to pick them up," remembers Karen Sprung. "We gave them an orientation on the bus including the history of Jamaica and a bit about our new resort.

FANFARE
Above: Welcoming guests is serious business for the Sandals team. Right: Guests enjoy cocktail hour.

All the Playmakers were dressed in uniforms: red polyester pants for girls, blue for boys, with a colorful pinstripe shirt. A band played in the lobby and everyone was just so thrilled to welcome these guests."

"I clearly remember the first dinner that evening," recalls Brian Roper, food and beverage manager at the time. "We had twenty-seven guests and forty-three dining room staff. Dinner took four and a half hours. Salad was served after the main course, and I don't believe dessert ever came out! We employed a very interesting chef at that time by the name of Percy Elliot, who worked best under the influence of white rum. Well, Percy and I sat down afterward in the kitchen, waiting to be let go. Mr. Stewart came in smiling and said, 'A job well done.' I knew my job was safe. We really had no clue at first, but it got better and better."

The rooms certainly offered the "wow" factor from the beginning. Guests were pleasantly surprised to find those special touches—king-size beds, clock radios and hair dryers.

THE FIRST GUESTS
Basil Cahusac, far right, turns on the charm, greeting the first guest with a kiss on the hand at the Montego Bay airport.

"But service was the real innovation," says David Roper. "Staff were encouraged to offer the service that they were trained for, but also to express their personality. So, for example, a bartender didn't stand behind the bar with his hands by his side waiting to be spoken to. He would open conversation with the guest."

Sandals Montego Bay General Manager Horace Peterkin agrees, "The position was: Forget about hotels and lead with hospitality. And that is what set Sandals apart."

It was exactly that attitude, work ethic and desire to please the customer that came forth—delivered straight from the appliance business, ATL.

"You see, Mr. Stewart did not bring a traditional hotelier's approach to running a resort," says David Roper. "Mr. Stewart taught me, and many others, that if guests want something, find a way to give it to them." He'd say to us, 'When someone comes to your hotel, forget that they're coming to your hotel. Pretend that they're coming to your house for a weekend and, what do you do the minute they come to your house, meet them outside with a big smile, bring them inside and offer them a drink and something to eat. Then take them to their bedroom. In other words, you treat them as your personal houseguests. Forget the fact that they're paying for it. Look on it as if it is a private invitation to your home. How would you treat your friends?' We thought, this is an interesting approach, a unique style. He molded us young guys in a new way, with a new approach. It's a philosophy that was never forgotten and a lot of us have adopted it and passed it down."

service

Robert "Daddy" Stone has played a pivotal role in shaping the services for which Sandals is renowned. He was hired as head maitre d' and was the resort's first staff employee in 1981.

"The hotel business is a people business and you have to please your customers. I have been with Sandals for more than twenty-three years and it makes me feel good to know that I was part of the original team that helped create the image of Sandals and that helped draw guests back again and again."

Beloved by staff and returning guests, Daddy Stone, now director of services, is considered the cornerstone of the flagship property.

**ROBERT "DADDY" STONE
DIRECTOR OF SERVICES
SANDALS MONTEGO BAY**

EVENING AT SANDALS: Mr. Basil Cahusac, Director of Entertainment, Activities and Public Relations at Sandals Resort Beach Club, Jamaica's newest resort, welcomes Mrs. Charles Sinclair (left), amd the Custos of St. James Mr. K.D. Henry and Mrs. Henry to a recent "Getting To Know Sandals" cocktail and dinner party. The party that was held for the Montego Bay business community was an opportunity for the management of Sandals to explain the concept behind the couples only, all inclusive resort.

Those that got the vision stayed and many, many remain with Sandals to this day. But in the beginning, finding the right general manger for Bay Roc proved to be a challenge. "While I was general manager at the Carlyle, Mr. Stewart couldn't keep any general manager at Bay Roc," remembers Merrick Fray. "So I used to do extra duties. If the general manager was gone, I used to go up there and manage the hotel until they found another general manager. One day Mr. Stewart said, 'You know, Merrick, you do better than all of these guys that I've brought in.' And I reminded him that in my initial interview I told him that if he wanted someone to manage both his hotels, I was his man. Within the week, he made me managing director." Quiet, unassuming, yet keenly effective, Merrick Fray is still at the helm as managing director today, obviously with the right attitude!

"In this business, you have to have the right attitude," says Robert Stone, who is now director of services. "When you hire people, you can tell from their behavior if they've got what it takes. You're looking for courtesy, someone who knows how to capably deal with people. You have to readjust yourself to cater to guests. We worked very hard at it and established Sandals in such a way that service became number one."

But it was a long haul to number one and by no means did success happen overnight. Indeed, Stewart and his team would have to work tirelessly and rely on an industry and its players that they were just beginning to understand. And so, with welcoming resort doors wide open, the Trader King-cum-hotelier set out on his brave new venture.

Aqua Sun Video & Photos

First on Film

Want to always recall the thrill of your first forty-foot scuba dive when you encountered a shipwreck off the coast of Negril? How about remembering the special dinner from your twenty-fifth wedding anniversary in Ocho Rios? Capturing precious times like these on film is best left to professionals. For forty-eight years, Aqua Sun Video and Photos, a Jamaica-based photography and video company, has taken memorable shots of vacationers at their best. Whether underwater while on a scuba diving or snorkeling trip or on land at an island wedding or family reunion, you can count on the team at Aqua Sun to be there in a snap to record and preserve magic moments. "Vacations are special times when people come together for happy occasions," says Stafford Subratie, managing director. "We are pleased to offer our services to Sandals' guests and to be there to capture all the memorable times for them."

"Cable & Wireless has ensured that the region continues to enjoy world-class telecommunications services by investing in the deployment of cutting-edge technologies."

GARY BARROW
PRESIDENT

Say

Cable & Wireless Jamaica is the leading provider of the island's domestic and international telephone services.

Cable & Wireless, one of the world's leading communications companies, provides voice, data and IP (Internet Protocol) services to business and residential customers, as well as services to other telecom carriers, mobile operators and providers of content, applications and Internet services.

The company's principal operations are in the United Kingdom, continental Europe, United States, Japan, Caribbean, Panama, Middle East, and Macau.

For over one hundred and thirty years, the company has, as necessary, reinvented itself to embrace the latest technological advances and to serve its customers' needs.

Top photos: Sandals Resorts International

"Hello"

Cable & Wireless has a history in the Caribbean that dates back to 1868. Over the years, Cable & Wireless has ensured that the region continues to enjoy world-class telecommunications services by investing in the deployment of cutting-edge technologies. The Cable & Wireless network across the region comprises digital microwave and submarine fiber cable systems backed by state-of-the-art network management and maintenance systems. This network delivers a comprehensive range of modern services unsurpassed for reliability.

In 2003, Cable & Wireless signaled that it would return to an earlier strategy that made it one of the major telecommunications companies in the world—focusing on operating national telephone companies, which traditionally enjoyed strong positions in their primary markets. These companies are closely bound by a common strategy; shared marketing, technical and regulatory skills; and established relationships both with each other and with national operators across the world.

Cable & Wireless Jamaica is the leading provider of the island's domestic and international telephone services. The company is also one of the leading providers of mobile services, with a recently installed GSM/GPRS mobile network, and was a pioneer in introducing mobile telephony to Jamaica in 1991. The company also offers a wide range of IP and Data Services and is the leading Internet Services Provider on the island.

Cable & Wireless Jamaica is a leader in corporate philanthropy, making large financial contributions to education, health, sports, and inner-city development. Some of the major beneficiaries have been the University Hospital of the West Indies; the Sickle Cell Education Centre; the University of the West Indies (UWI); the University of Technology (UTech); The National Foundation for Science and Technology; and the Multi-Care Foundation, a private sector-funded organization established to improve social conditions and provide self-improvement opportunities for inner-city youth.

The company is also the major and title sponsor of the national High Schools Lawn Tennis Competition; the island's Badminton Program; and the Jamaica Senior National Netball Team.

Cable & Wireless Jamaica has also been on two occasions a major sponsor of the island's national soccer team, The Reggae Boyz, and, in 2003, was the naming and title sponsor for the Cable & Wireless World Netball Championships, which was held in the capital city, Kingston.

In addition, the company has adopted three primary schools in rural Jamaica. And, Cable & Wireless makes hundreds of small donations to a plethora of other organizations.

3 Keeping Company

NONE OF US HAD EVER SEEN THAT MANY TRAVEL AGENTS COME THROUGH HOTELS. I THINK NOWHERE BEFORE HAD ANY HOTEL BEEN EXPOSED TO THE TRAVEL TRADE LIKE THIS. OUR MARKETING VIEW WAS QUITE SIMPLE: UNLESS YOU SHOW YOUR PRODUCT YOU'LL NEVER GET ANY-ONE TO SELL IT.

Merrick Fray
Managing Director
Sandals Resorts International

One evening…

at dusk a few months after Sandals Resort Beach Club opened, entertainment director Basil Cahusac and Butch Stewart were walking along the beach. A plane roared above them. Sandals, or "Hangar 109," as some locals referred to the resort, had become the brunt of many jokes. Stewart was not amused. He groused, "Basil, this damn airport is giving me trouble. What are we going to do about the planes flying overhead?" Cahusac replied, "Give me a week or so to come up with something."

"They took this old **battered-up** place and really *turned it around.*"

POSITIVE REACTION

Cahusac watched guest reactions when planes took off: Sometimes fists shot up in the air, sometimes so did the finger. He thought, why not take that negative energy and convert it to something positive. Make lemonade from this lemon. Why not turn it into a wave? Then, he made it far more interesting. Sandals quickly adopted Cahusac's imaginative and much-loved practice: "Every time a plane flies overhead, you must wave and kiss the person you came with," Cahusac and the Playmakers instructed guests. "Everyone got into *that*," recalls Cahusac, "especially the honeymooners and those getting married. You must make a negative into a positive and it was the easiest thing to do."

Indeed, early skeptics, even those well established in the tourism industry, were impressed. Anthony Abrahams, former minister of tourism for Jamaica, visited the property a few months after it had opened: "I recall the first time I went to tour the new all-inclusive. I have to admit that I was a little cynical and skeptical and curious, of course. I heard Butch had spent some money on it, but I also knew the hotel had a terrible problem in that every time a plane took off it veered left over the hotel and made the most god-awful noise. So, I am sitting there by the pool and every time a plane went overhead, I see people happily waving hands up in the air at it like a bunch of lunatics, mad people. And I sat there and I watched this and realized that what they have really done is taken a major negative and made something positive. Obviously he saw an opportunity; and that, to me, is one of the things that sums up Butch Stewart's success: the ability to, out of adversity, see and create opportunity. They took this old battered-up place and really turned it around."

ASK ME WHERE I'D *Rather* BE! *Sandals* All-Inclusive Club Resorts

LOVE IS IN THE AIR

Left: Entertainment director Basil Cahusac, seated front, is surrounded by Sandals Playmakers. Opposite: Lovebirds at Sandals Montego Bay kiss for the camera.

Stewart and his team didn't do it alone. They relied on some of the most indispensable tools in the industry—wholesalers, tour operators and travel agents. "We've had a love affair with travel agents from the very beginning," beams Stewart. "And they remain more relevant today than ever before."

Before falling head over heels, however, Stewart had to get acquainted with the industry players, to understand them and how the business worked. With gusto, he immersed himself in the trade, asking questions, educating himself, and depending on those in the know, including George Myers, who was known as "Mr. Tourism" and was the recipient of the 1980 Caribbean Hotel Association Hotelier of the Year award.

"Butch came to see me shortly after he purchased Bay Roc," says Myers, president of The Myers Group. "We were friends from way back, and at that time I was heading up Resorts International in Nassau. He was determined to get involved and learn the hotel business. I shared my insight with him and advised him to fly up to New York and introduce himself to tour operators, folks like Joe Garzilli from Flyfaire and Fred Kassner from GOGO Tours."

"What's a Butch Stewart? That was the reaction we had at Flyfaire when we first heard about this guy," said Warren Cohen, when he worked for the number one Caribbean wholesaler at that time. "Nobody knew him. Our thought was: Oh well, look at this guy who's in the appliance business, knows nothing about hotels, and buys a run-down hotel at the end of a runway. Nobody knew Butch. But he came to town with personality to spare; he's an extremely charismatic individual. I think when he first came to New York, everybody was sort of attracted to this very extroverted Jamaican guy. I don't know how seriously they took him, but people eventually bought into what he was saying. The thought was, yes, he's a colorful character, Myers is vouching for him, what do we have to lose? We'll work with the guy."

butchspeaks

WHEN BUTCH STEWART SPEAKS, PEOPLE LISTEN. HERE'S HOW TO INTERPRET HIS LINGO:

"Hi, sexy"	= I can't remember your name.
"Talk fast"	= I'm tired of listening to you talk rubbish.
"Watch me now"	= Listen carefully and comply.
"Trust me"	= Do not even think of arguing.
"You're knocking on an open door"	= Yes. Do it.
"No ifs, buts or maybes"	= We're starting construction now and opening the hotel in three months.

BUSINESS AND FINANCE

What they say about Sandals!

Marcia Erskine looks at two U.S. features

Sandals- the Montego Bay Beach Resort- has in recent times been earning much positive publicity in a number of foreign publications.

The prestigious U.S. "Travel Weekly" last month described the transformation of the former Bay Roc Resort into the Sandals Resort Beach Club as "nothing short of miraculous".

The Weekly's travel writer Joel Glass, said that "the renaissance at the property is a reflection of Jamaica itself since the change of Government in October 1980 triggered a wave of refurbishings of the island's physical plant."

Tracing what he termed "the long slide toward neglect" of the former Bay Roc Hotel, Glass described Sandals as "a new product that is drawing a lot of attention and business."

Glass found particular pleasure in the property's "geodesic skydome in the center of the main building

where a garden held sway in Bay Roc days" but where a large semi-circular show-area for nighttime, open-air entertainment is now "surrounded by Jamaican pink Trelawny stone".

Glass's sto. was a literal tour aroun. Sandals touching on the resort's pool area, health club, tennis courts and the beach itself.

This latter, he said, was one of Sandals' main selling points. He likened life at the resort to a journey on a cruise ship :"virtually every hour of every day has some sort of planned activity on a take-it or leave-it basis".

The Jax Fax Travel Marketing Magazine in Connecticut also had much praise for Sandals. They devoted 5-pages to what they headlined " The Confessions of a Closet Clubbie... or how I Discovered - and was Discovered -at Sandals".

Written by Mona

Moore, a self-confessed "non-joiner by nature" who had "never been big on the all-inclusive club-style vacation concept", Moore said that she was however, tempted to go to Sandals because of an urge to get to the sun and the attraction of the idea of the being at a resort that would offer her the whole gamut of beach sports.

Another attraction, she said, was the fact that Sandals was designed for couples. So, she figured, if all else failed, her " partner in crime" could offer enough distraction from "the boring 'r.zos" she expected to meet.

Moore was impressed by the bellman at Sandals who on their arrival not only showed them efficiently to their rooms but refused a tip,in keeping with the hotel's all inclusive policy.

Another plus, she thought, was the "delightful - spacious and airy - rooms, each with its own separate balcony that looks over the ocean".

Moore was pleasantly surprised that meal time was no buffet affair but rather, featured " a maitre'd dressed to the gills" who showed them to

a-linen-covered table.

"There was no buffet line, no waiting for drinks tha never came... the drinks were served by one waiter, the main course by another, and the side dishes by a third - all in rapid succession. It was a rare and pleasurable experience- particularly in the Caribbean."

Moore described her stay at Sandals as one in "a virtual paradise" consisting of "a wonderful room, a good friend to share it with, three more than adequate 'squares a day', and a world of entertainment" at her disposal.

She found pleasure in the sporting and other activities, and the specially laid-out nighttime entertainment she found pleasantly "polished". She summed up her pleasure: These people were good, not just costumes fluff".

By the time M vaction was up, she fessed, she left " much verbal protest newly converted but fi. loyal, dues paying mem of Sandals".

With an endorsement like that, it seems pretty certain this lady will be back for more.

Butch Stewart?"

"We were located in a tiny office," recalls Jean Jutan, then vice president of sales and marketing. "An 800 number was set up and we were in business. It was a secretary-reservations gal and myself. Good thing, because we couldn't even move in that space! It was twelve feet by three feet, packed to the hilt with boxes of brochures and such. You could hardly move, but boy did we work those phones to get the word out about Sandals."

Stewart's executive assistant, Betty Jo Desnoes, recalls that Stewart would make regular calls to all the travel agents and tour operators. "He established personal relationships with them to become special to them, and they were special to him. It was a higher level of relationship than just a business relationship. And that is what he really achieved with all of them."

STARTING OUT
Far left: A young Stewart emerges. Left: The cover of Sandals' first brochure. Top: Sandals receives good press coverage.

FAST FRIENDS
George Myers, a well-regarded Caribbean hotelier and businessman, right, helped teach Stewart the ropes in the early days. Inset photo: Myers, circa 1962, was Stewart's roommate.

> "We're a mass-marketer of travel and we love to sell Sandals. It's a fabulous product and our clients enjoy the Sandals experience."
>
> MICHELLE KASSNER
> PRESIDENT

Pioneers of

Kassner and Haroche were two of the first believers in the all-inclusive concept.

Fashioning
GoGo's New World

GoGo Worldwide Vacations sets a new course that takes advantage of the business savvy of President Fred Kassner (center), the fresh vision of Senior Vice President-Marketing Michelle Kassner (right) and the experience of Vice President Michael Norton

Sales Guides
Inside: Domestic Tour Manual ▪ Section Two: Europe
Section Three: Pacific/Asia ▪ Section Four: Ski Colorado
Section Five: YP&B/Yankelovich Partners 1996 National Travel Monitor
Exclusive Insert: Florida Vacation Specialist Course, Lesson 2

Sandals Regency St. Lucia Golf Resort & Spa

the Package Vacation

The slogan of the National Association of Travel Officials, "You've earned your vacation—now enjoy it," originated in 1946, which the organization declared as "Victory Vacation Year." At the time, America had entered a new post-war era where leisure vacations and travel became more important and more valued by everyone. By the mid-1950s, nearly half the United States population took vacations each year. Escape, travel and fun were what people wanted. Tropical beaches were beckoning them.

Two New York University graduates who became young travel agents in New York City saw an opportunity and seized it. In 1951, Fred Kassner and Gilbert Haroche set up operations, known as Liberty Travel and Keystone Tours, in a tiny one-room office in Times Square. They set out to offer the glamour and appeal of top destinations like Miami Beach to those who would normally drive to a nearby beach or lake.

Kassner worked the phones and visited suppliers, negotiating bulk rates. Through his tenacity, creativity and business acumen, he developed the vacation package concept. For the first time, consumers could purchase a package that included air fare, hotel and transportation. The company, by then known as GOGO Tours, built its business on vacations in which the total

Sandals Grande St. Lucian Spa & Beach Resort

cost of the trip's inclusions was less expensive as a package than the sum of the individual components would be. The traveling public bought in to this packaged vacation concept, and the company started by Kassner and Haroche grew into one of the largest travel companies in the United States.

GOGO was among the first wholesalers to package vacations to Florida and to Puerto Rico. Over the years, the company expanded its vacation offerings, selling packages to Mexico and to the Caribbean. When Jamaica's all-inclusive hotels started to sprout, Kassner and Haroche were two of the first believers in the concept. So when Butch Stewart was starting to sell his new all-inclusive resort, he turned to GOGO Tours. Stewart met Kassner and the two hit it off.

"Butch and Fred had a mutual respect for each other," says Michelle Kassner, president of GOGO Worldwide Vacations and the daughter of the late Fred Kassner. "Butch bounced a lot of ideas and thoughts off of Fred. He looked up to him and regarded his opinion."

As Sandals continued to grow over the years, its relationship with GOGO Worldwide Vacations became stronger. Today, the two companies remain as close as ever. "GOGO and Sandals are basically family," says Warren Cohen, senior vice president of marketing and sales development for Unique Vacations. Indeed, GOGO sends in excess of fifty thousand customers every year to Sandals and Beaches resorts.

GOGO Worldwide Vacations recently celebrated its fiftieth year in business, and today the company is thriving under the direction of Michelle Kassner. GOGO remains the largest

privately owned wholesaler of leisure vacations, as well as the top producer in the industry and one of the top wholesalers to the Caribbean, Florida and Mexico. The company serves more than eighteen thousand travel agencies in the United States and has more than forty neighborhood offices in twenty-four states of the United States.

Despite its tremendous growth, the company stays true to its ideals and traditions. Friendly professionalism and personal service mark the GOGO brand, which continues to stand by its core values: offering affordable worldwide travel programs, providing top service, taking a hometown approach to business, and working exclusively with travel agents.

As a company formed by two travel agents, GOGO has always believed in the value of the individual travel agent. "In a world of rapid changes and shifting loyalties, agents remain a constant for us at GOGO," says Michelle Kassner. "Our success is directly related to the agency distribution system. And, agents consistently turn to us because we provide no-assembly-required packages, needing only one call or contact, to offer their clients a complete vacation program."

GOGO vacation programs and packages are available to two hundred destinations on four continents, and include the Caribbean, Central America, Europe, Florida, Hawaii, Las Vegas, Mexico, and Tahiti. The company has long-standing relationships with the most well-respected brands in the hospitality industry, making it easy to do business. Packages also come with an exclusive warranty for travel agents and an optional travel protection plan for travelers.

Though a powerful industry force, GOGO Worldwide Vacations conducts business with a neighborhood approach. Michelle Kassner recalls, "My father saw the value of developing local markets by providing personalized service within the community and we continue that today. Regionally, we are viewed as a small hometown office."

Always innovators, GOGO has put a strong focus on developing technology. "We are very committed to e-business," says Michelle Kassner. "With the growing preference by agents to book on the Internet, we've invested heavily in enhancing our Web site, making it faster and easier for agents to market, to sell and to keep informed about our products."

The Halloran House, at 525 Lexington Avenue, between 48th and 49th streets, was the site of Sandals' first press conference in September 1981. Members of the travel trade and tour operators were in attendance. It was a big deal, and Jean Jutan wanted Butch Stewart to appear as a serious hotelier. "This was our formal debut and we had to make the right impression," says Jutan. "Well, Butch came to town in his bell-bottom polyester pants and cowboy boots. It was just part of his casual, relaxed demeanor. I cried, 'No way. You can't come to the conference dressed like that! You have to exude richness and sophistication.' So I took him on a New York shopping trip to outfit him properly. Of course, once he got up to speak, it didn't matter what he was wearing. He was, and is, the consummate salesman and best spokesperson for Sandals because he so absolutely believes in the product that he's selling."

**Above: General Manager Baldwin Powell boogies down.
Right: Entertaining travel agents has always been a favorite pastime at Sandals.**

"We were told quite frankly,'You have a party. You make sure you have a party.'"

Jutan was off and running, attending travel trade shows. Early deals were signed at the Caribbean Tourist Association's Marketplace '82 at the Inter-Continental Hotel in Ocho Rios, among other shows. And, Sandals began bringing travel agents down to Jamaica for familiarization trips, or FAMs, knowing they had to have agents experience the property firsthand.

"From day one, travel agents came to the properties in large numbers, says Merrick Fray, managing director for Sandals Resorts International. "None of us had ever seen that many travel agents come through hotels. I think nowhere before had any hotel been exposed to the travel trade like this. Our marketing view was quite simple: Unless you show your product, you'll never get anyone to sell it."

David Roper concurs, "We were told quite frankly, 'You have a party. You make sure you have a party.' Our job was to make sure that travel agents staying at our properties had the most incredible experience. I recall one time when it was raining, I went into the pool fully clothed to create a party. And we called it our wet fete! It was good, clean fun."

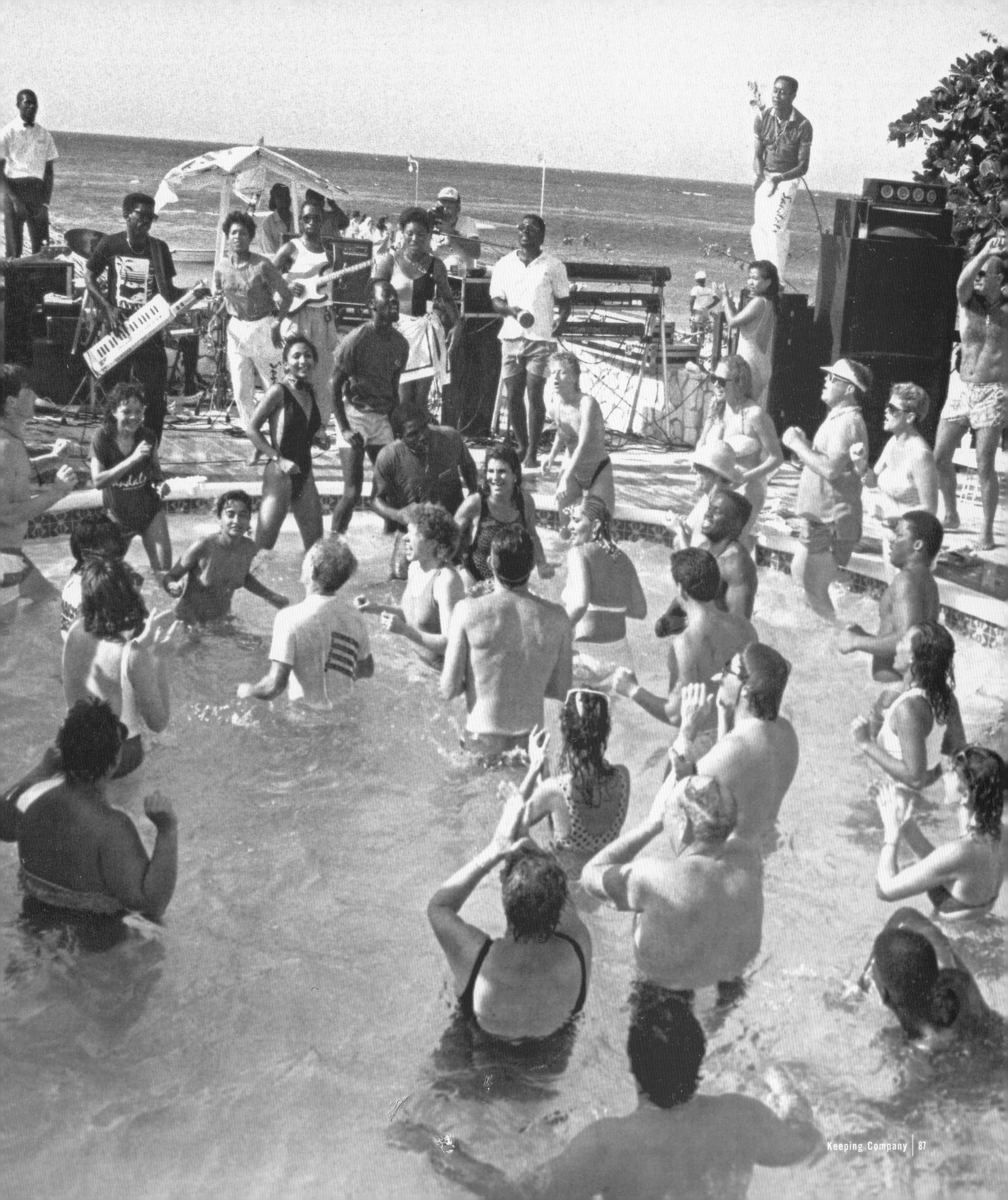

Here Comes the Bride

Bridal Guide magazine is a leader in the bridal market with nearly one million unduplicated readers, the most in-depth editorial around, and the ability to reach engaged couples in print, in person and online. What began as a small digest-sized publication in 1981 has grown to become the standard in industry innovation, with polybagged issues, pocked-sized planning guides, a *Honeymoon Guide* magazine supplement, and more.

Bridal Guide's editorial focuses intensely on travel and honeymoons, making it an ideal venue for the Sandals message. In fact, *Bridal Guide* and Sandals have had a successful partnership for more than fifteen years, with *Bridal Guide* featuring the resorts in sweepstakes and other promotional endeavors, and teaming up to sponsor The Great Bridal Expo, which is the largest touring bridal exhibition in the United States.

"Our mission is to give our readers what they want and need to plan their dream wedding and honeymoon," says Tom Curtin, senior vice president and publisher of *Bridal Guide*. "We also want to give our advertisers the best, most targeted and cost-effective way to reach our market. Ideally, those goals coincide where advertisers' messages fulfill readers' needs. That is certainly true with Sandals— the absolute leader in honeymoons and destination weddings."

> *"Our mission is to give readers what they want and need to plan their dream wedding and honeymoon."*
>
> TOM CURTIN
> SENIOR VICE PRESIDENT AND PUBLISHER

CONCRETE SOLUTIONS

Feedback from those travel agents, other industry partners and hotel guests prompted the Sandals team to quickly get working on property enhancements. "We invest in people and concrete," one of Stewart's mantras, meant more innovations would soon come. "The product was extremely primitive at first," recalls Warren Cohen, then a tour operator with Flyfaire, who is now senior vice president of marketing and sales development for Unique Vacations. "But Butch learns fast and has a tremendous commitment to product, and he isn't afraid to go in and spend money to differentiate his product from other all-inclusives."

In 1983, just as Sandals Resort Beach Club was starting to grow in popularity, a series of groundbreaking upgrades were revealed. A new sixty-six-room Palms block offered guests true beachfront rooms on that gorgeous stretch of beach. A fitness center was built amid tropical Japanese fishponds covered by wooden bridges and garden sitting areas. The facility housed a Universal Training System, exercise bikes and saunas. The water-sports program was upgraded, with scuba diving, snorkeling and waterskiing added as all-inclusive amenities. And for the first time in the Caribbean, Jacuzzis became part of the hotel landscape. Sandals placed several of the steamy whirlpools within the perfumed gardens.

TO KEEP FIT, one has to undertake an exercise programme that is meant to be successful; but to achieve this goal, one also has to have a combination of willpower, and good & useful equipment. Recently, Sandals Resort Beach Club, Montego Bay, invited the President of the JHTA, Mr. Godfrey Dyer, and members of the local press, to a Press Conference and Luncheon as well as a tour of their facilities. Everyone was impressed with what they saw - a T.V. satellite dish, two cold storage rooms, specially built to hold large quantities of perishable food; converted deluxe rooms and a well-equipped gym, saunas & hot tubs. Here, Mr. Richard Michelin (left) General Manager of Sandals Resort Beach Club, Mr. 'Butch' Stewart, of Appliance Traders Group of Companies, look on appreciatively, as Mr. Godfrey Dyer, President of the Jamaica Hotel & Tourist Association and Mrs. Norma Taylor, PRO/Writer, Jamaica Tourist Board, check out their gym equipment. —JTB Photo.

SPIN CYCLE
Staff members and Stewart, second from left, check out the new Universal Training System fitness equipment, installed in 1983.

Then food and beverage manager Brian Roper recalls of Stewart, "There wasn't a week when we never saw him. He got to know all of the staff. He ate in the staff canteen and mixed with all the guests. And he listened to what everyone had to say. I think, more than anything, what we picked up was the energy and the vision that he had. We all took a cue from that. Look, if this person can work 24/7 with that amount of enthusiasm, it does rub off down the line."

swim on up

The following year, a novelty was created that would long be associated with Sandals: the swim-up pool bar, designed by architect Evan Williams. "We recently had built the Palms block at the far end of the property and wanted something to attract guests to that area," says Williams. "As architect for an all-inclusive resort, I wanted to create a sense of someone leaving their room and going to a destination within the property, making an interesting transition between spaces. We also wanted to spread out activity and thought it would be nice to have another pool. But, how do you make it exciting enough to have people walk all the way down to that pool? There was nothing

in that previous space, so the concept was to create a relic, a new facility that looked like it had been there forever. Butch and I were having a discussion and I remarked, 'I never understood why you couldn't have bars in pools.' Butch said, 'Well, it's never been done. Let's give it a shot. Use your imagination.'" Williams designed the lagoon-shaped pool bar with stools built right into the water next to a full-service bar. The guests went wild for the concept. And today it remains a standard feature at all Sandals and Beaches resorts.

"Unless you show your product you'll never get anyone to sell it."

GETTING ASSOCIATED

Especially in those early years, Sandals devised many appealing features for its all-inclusive product. It also made mistakes along the way. "The first two years were rough, and it wasn't until a couple of years into the thing before we came to grips with the situation and slowly started turning things around," says Stewart. "Yes, at times it was frustrating; but rather than reduce our involvement, we invested more. It paid off."

These new hotel recruits were eager to learn the business and grow with it. In fact, from early on, Stewart took an active leadership role in the industry. In 1984, Butch Stewart was named president of the Jamaica Hotel and Tourist Association (JHTA). "He brought a whole new style and flair into the JHTA," notes John Lynch, former deputy director of the Jamaica Tourist Board and now executive vice president of sales worldwide for Unique Vacations.

"The JHTA went from a dormant association to becoming very proactive in terms of marketing with the tourist board, supporting Jamaica's small hotels and inns, and rallying the government to cause positive change for the tourism product," says Lynch.

Stewart's executive assistant, Betty Jo Desnoes, concurs, "As president of the JHTA, he brought hoteliers together. With the power of many, he went to the Jamaican government asking for incentives for the hotel industry so that it could improve the product, especially for the small hotels. His philosophy has always been to assist the small hoteliers because it diversifies the product in Jamaica."

NEW PRESIDENT FOR JHTA

NEW JHTA PRESIDENT: Mr. Gordon "Butch" Stewart (center) newly elected President of the Jamaica Hotel and Tourist Association (JHTA) shortly after giving his first presidential address. Flanking him are Director of Tourism Ms. Carrole Guntley and Minister of State for Tourism Dr. Marco Brown. Stewart is chairman of Sandals, the all-inclusive resort for couples and the Carlyle Hotel, both in Montego Bay.

SHOW OFFS
Left: Stewart, middle, stayed active as president of the Jamaica Hotel and Tourist Association, serving four consecutive years, and as a marketer of his new hotel. Above: Sandals launches innovative displays to attract guests.

" MR. STEWART EXPLAINED HIS VISION OF SALES, AND WE LEARNED HOW IMPORTANT TRAVEL AGENTS WERE. WE SHOWED THEM AROUND THE HOTEL, TOOK THEM DANCING, AND ESCORTED THEM ON TOURS. IN THE DAYS WHEN MR. STEWART USED TO SELL AIR CONDITIONERS, IT WAS ALL BASED ON HONESTY AND HARD WORK. HE WOULD GET AN ORDER FOR AN AIR CONDITIONER AND HAVE HIS GUYS GO TO THE HOUSE, BANG A HOLE IN THE WALL AND YOU'D HAVE YOUR AIR CONDITIONER THAT NIGHT. AND HE'S ALWAYS HAD THAT ATTITUDE. HE SAYS TO A TRAVEL AGENT, SEND ME YOUR CLIENTS AND I'LL LOOK AFTER THEM. IT'S THE SAME PHILOSOPHY. "

Brian Roper
Group Director of Operations
Sandals Resorts International

Keeping Travelers Happy

**Butch Stewart and Carla Stratton
of Happy Vacations**

For thirty-five years, Happy Vacations has had a single focus: to offer the best vacation product with the highest caliber of service in an effort to keep customers content. That's how the company has kept its customers so satisfied all these years. "Our business is built on the principles of integrity, excellence, innovation, and customer service," says Rick Garrett, president. "Our work is to build solid relationships with all of our customers, whether they be travel agents, travelers or industry partners. Furthermore, we strive to provide the finest products and the most knowledgeable staff."

Happy Vacation's decades-long partnership with Sandals has been based on those same values. Both companies have centered their success on customer relationships. Collaborative efforts between the two include product education, trendsetting marketing, advertising initiatives, and cutting-edge travel technology. "Butch Stewart and his incredible team have kept the partnership lively and productive," says Dorothy Morgan, director of marketing. "They've gone above and beyond to show their appreciation for us as travel partners, and together we've been able to form a very strong synergy."

By 1985, rock-solid relationships with tour operators and travel agents had been established. "I remember when we had one of our first award ceremonies in recognition of our travel partners," recalls Merrick Fray. "We were just taken aback by the level of support that this one hotel received in what was a recovering Caribbean island at best. People like Fred Kassner of GOGO Tours, Joe Garzilli of Flyfaire, and Bob Grinberg of Globetrotters were there.

"They really took Mr. Stewart under their wing. Those tour operators were present at every major function and at every recognition award we sponsored. Every time Mr. Stewart needed help, he could call on them. He's a natural builder of relationships and he really worked the relationships and they became much more than just business partners."

Fray continues: "The relationship with GOGO Tours, now GOGO Worldwide Vacations, is extraordinary. Fred Kassner was like a surrogate father to Mr. Stewart. A couple of days didn't go by that he wouldn't be on

Top: Sandals' longtime staff members enjoy a night out at Sandals Montego Bay.

the phone calling him up, 'Sir Fred, so how do you do this, or what do you think of that?' Mr. Kassner was a king in the travel industry. His companies supply more business to the Caribbean than any other organization. He was conservative and reserved in demeanor, but he had his attention to detail.

"In the early days, I recall that Mr. Kassner could reel off all the Sandals inclusions right down to the bedside clock radios, even though we only had one hotel. He became a believer in the concept from the early days, from before Sandals had all the marble and pretty finishes, when it was just a basic three-star hotel. He and the entire GOGO team really evolved with Sandals as we went on to become an ultra all-inclusive."

TRYING SANDALS ON FOR SIZE

Gordon Stewart (left), owner of Sandals Resort Beach Club, Jamaica, and president of the Jamaican Hotel and Tourist Association, shows Joe Garzilli, president of Flyfaire, Inc., some of the attractions at his resort. Sandals is designed for adult couples only and has an all-inclusive, pre-paid policy. All rooms in the 219-room property are air conditioned and have king-size beds, telephones, and balconies or patios.

Sandals first jet flown by longtime pilot Captain Johnny Harris.

By 1986, the concept Sandals was selling caught on. Sandals Resort Beach Club had become a fine-tuned hotel with a reputation as the *in* place to play in Jamaica, especially for honeymooners. "Actually it took us from 1981 to 1986 to get the formulas and behavior and the management that became a kind of standard. We may not have invented the all-inclusive concept but, because of the innovations and the high caliber of our product, we really perfected it," says Stewart. Sandals was on a roll. The time for expansion had arrived.

But why expand? Here is this winning businessman running a successful appliance business and now a popular resort. Why not sit back and relax? "Butch is never going to sit still," says Warren Cohen. "He's always going to evolve, progress and move forward. Butch is not one to say, 'Hey this is great, let's put our feet up.' He's always looking for the next challenge, the next opportunity."

There was tremendous demand for the product. Guests wanted the relaxed vibe and romance that was Sandals. "Mr. Stewart's vision was correct," notes architect Evan Williams. "In the early 1980s, the all-inclusive market was still vague in terms of what it meant. What Sandals did in those early days—and continues to do to this day—was to create a resort that not only had ambiance but also what it takes to get a guest to return again and again."

Tortuga Rum Company Ltd.

Success is Sweet

In 1984, Robert Hamaty, a former Air Jamaica captain, and his wife, Carlene, founded Tortuga Rum Company on Grand Cayman. They started with two rums, Tortuga Gold Rum and Tortuga Light Rum, which are specially blended using Jamaican and Barbadian rums.

Carlene started baking rum cakes using a one-hundred-year-old family recipe. Tortuga Gold Rum was her special ingredient. Today, the company operates a ten-thousand-square-foot, state-of-the-art bakery producing up to ten thousand rum cakes per day. And the Hamatys are credited as pioneers in developing a global awareness of Caribbean fancy foods.

From its inception twenty years ago, Tortuga Rum Company has grown to become the largest duty-free liquor business in the Cayman Islands. The name has also become synonymous with one of the world's finest confections: the authentic Tortuga Rum Cake, which is the Cayman Island's top souvenir.

Although Tortuga Rum Cake is world-famous, the recipe remains a secret.

A Bottle of Red

The sound of popping corks enlivens the evening hours at all Sandals and Beaches restaurants. Chilean cabernet? French pinot noir? The wine cellar contains a variety of delicious wines to sip and swirl.

Arosa Limited, Jamaica's largest purveyors of fine wines, has played sommelier at the Sandals and Beaches properties for several years, providing an array of wines to meet the needs of discerning guests. "We carry wines from all over the world, including Australia, Italy, France, Switzerland, Spain, and California," says Robert Hoehener, Arosa's chairman and managing director.

Hoehener started Arosa Limited in 1986. In those days, the company focused on producing a variety of fine meats manufactured to the highest international standards, which allowed the company to export to a number of other countries. From the beginning, the company was committed to producing and supplying the best of the best. Its successful growth led it to expand. Several years ago, in response to client requests, Arosa ventured into the wine market with a small selection of wines. The selection and quality of offerings were impressive, and the wine business grew rapidly.

> ## "We are proud to meet the needs of Jamaica's finest all-inclusive group."
>
> ROBERT HOEHENER
> CHAIRMAN AND MANAGING DIRECTOR

Butch Stewart flanked by Sandals chefs

Recently, Arosa entered into the dairy market with select cheeses and other fine dairy products. Bring on the goat cheese canapés and pour the shiraz!

SANDALS GETS STATELY

The Royal Caribbean Hotel, left and below, was highly regarded for its quiet elegance.

A PAIR OF SANDALS

Just a mile down the road from Sandals Resort Beach Club was the Royal Caribbean Hotel, another fantastic resort in its day. Stewart acquired the property in 1986 and quickly started renovations.

"I had been working at the Royal Caribbean Hotel since 1984," recalls Sandals General Manager Baldwin Powell. "My impression was that the Royal was one of the better hotels to work for. We had very good occupancies, nice rooms and facilities, and a great restaurant. When Sandals officially took over in April 1986, I was assistant manager in charge of the rooms division, then working along with David Roper, who was the general manager. Sandals came in and started to tear out everything. They gutted rooms, retiled bathrooms, added new carpet, brought in new furniture, and placed Jacuzzis all around."

"We had the Flyfaire sales meeting on property literally the day that Sandals Royal Caribbean opened in April," recalls Warren Cohen. "Well, the hotel was not one hundred percent complete. But over the course of our four-day meeting, an astonishing metamorphosis took place. Every time we'd come out of the conference room for a break, you'd see another completed improvement to the hotel. So, at eleven o'clock, you'd find one hundred deck chairs that had not been there an hour before placed all around the pool."

Recalls David Roper, "When we opened, Sandals Resort Beach Club changed its name to Sandals Montego Bay in order to distinguish it from Sandals Royal Caribbean. We soon came to understand the philosophy and what Sandals was about in terms of creating and developing innovations, particularly in the area of food and dining."

"We truly revolutionized the all-inclusive food concept."

RESTAURANT REVOLUTION

In the early years, food and restaurant choices were very basic. Sandals Resort Beach Club opened with one restaurant serving breakfast and lunch buffets. The dinner menu was very simple: two soups, one salad and three entrées. Soon enough, the hotels inaugurated the now-common specialty dining concept with formal service and high culinary standards.

"Serving fresh tropical fruits was synonymous with the Caribbean," says David Roper. "I can recall very early on that Mr. Stewart decided he wanted his guests to have fresh fruit available by the beach. At any other hotel, you would simply find a small bit of cut-up fruit served on a plate. Mr. Stewart had different ideas. He thought, let's display the fruit and give guests a different experience with a real Caribbean flair. 'Go find a way to do it.' So off we went to a nearby fishing village where we found an old wooden canoe. We cleaned it up, painted it up and set it up on the beach under two thatched huts. We filled it with ice and loaded it with tropical fruit all cut up. Guests would go and help themselves. Nowhere in the Caribbean was this done. That was an interesting notion and all of us were constantly searching for progressive ways to upgrade the food and dining."

"However, the advent of specialty dining really came about just by chance," claims Merrick Fray. "I had read somewhere that Club Med was contemplating having a dining area that was not their regular buffet. I went to my assistant at the time, Freddie Marsh, and said, 'Why can't we do something like this?' We came up with the specialty restaurant concept and went to Mr. Stewart. He said, 'Yes, try it.' The Oleander, set on the verandah at Sandals Montego Bay, became the very first specialty restaurant and served Jamaican cuisine. It only had about twelve seats, but it was very popular."

The Oleander was such a hit with guests that soon after Sandals Royal Caribbean installed a specialty restaurant. "The all-inclusives had a reputation for buffet breakfasts, lunches and dinners. When travel agents sent their guests down for a week, it was twenty-one buffet meals," said Brian Roper. "So we truly revolutionized the all-inclusive food concept by introducing gourmet restaurants with signature white-glove service and exotic specialty dining by reservation only."

Larry Kline Wholesale Meats

Bon Appétit

The Sandals team took the concept of gourmet dining to new heights when they opened the Oleander, the first specialty restaurant. As the company continued opening resorts, guests expected the cuisine to be as impressive as the surroundings.

Soon, premium-brand filet mignon, veal chops and rack of lamb all made their way to the table to tantalize tastebuds thanks to Larry Kline Meats, purveyors of quality meats and provisions. Four brothers form the management team. Each learned the business from his parents, Larry and Lois, who started the business in 1976.

"Larry Kline founded his company based on the principles of providing top-notch service and quality products. Today, we serve an impressive list of clients, including fine hotels, restaurants and country clubs in South Florida and the Caribbean," says Steve Caine, director of operations.

Pesto-glazed rack of lamb. Braised pork medallions with mangoes in port. Roasted duck breast with caramelized orange sauce. They are all tempting selections on the menu at Sandals and Beaches resorts.

JAMAICA
Make it fun, carefree
and adventurous.
Make it Jamaica. Again.

DESTINATION: JAMAICA

Nineteen eighty-seven was a banner year
for Caribbean tourism. Jamaica was one of
the greatest beneficiaries, hosting its one-
millionth visitor that year. Credit goes to the
tourism machine of hoteliers with fabulous
hotel offerings, travel agents and tour operators
who supported the destination, and tourism
officials who helped encourage and promote
Jamaica as a top vacation spot. It was during
this climate of growth and booming business
that Butch Stewart, the true entrepreneur,
chose to spread his wings once more.

"Jamaica is by far the most beautiful
country in the world," proudly boasts Stewart
of his homeland. "It's an island with far
more potential than even the people living
here realize. Every
mile of coastline is an
opportunity and a
possible attraction."

COAST TO COAST
Butch Stewart loved the
beaches of Negril so much that
he could not resist buying two
old neighboring resorts in the
area in 1987. After a year of
construction, Sandals Negril,
at right, opened.

That said, Stewart bought two old neighboring hotels, the Coconut Cove Beach Hotel and the Sundowner, situated on the loveliest slice of Negril's famed seven-mile, white-sand beach. Ground-breaking for Sandals Negril took place on February 25, 1988, with Jamaica's then prime minister, Edward Seaga, as special guest, along with scores of fellow hoteliers, tourism and government officials, and foreign and local press on hand. The event was a huge success, but construction on the site, which would merge the two older properties into one, proved to be long and strenuous, with a few unwelcome surprises along the way.

Stewart and the Sandals team would soon find out that, indeed, love is all you need.

Cairsea Services

All's Clear

In 1974, when Rodney Thompson arrived on Providenciales in the Turks and Caicos Islands, there were no telephones, no newspapers, no radios. In fact, there were fewer than one thousand residents.

"The island was a retreat for the adventurous few who enjoyed simple pleasures and an unencumbered lifestyle," recalls Thompson.

Thompson and his wife, Sharon, began their freight and customs brokerage business by selling goods from the cargo door of an old DC-3 aircraft. As the island developed, hotels and companies needed reliable brokerage services.

One Sunday, a new dive boat arrived for a film shoot with no advance notice. It was a scramble, but Cairsea cleared the vessel and the shoot went ahead on schedule.

Today, imports ranging from food to furniture are cleared through Cairsea, the Thompson's company.

"We're the buffer between fantasy and reality."

RODNEY THOMPSON
OWNER

"GORDON 'BUTCH' STEWART, FOUNDER AND OWNER OF THE SANDALS CHAIN OF HOTELS IS A HOUSEHOLD NAME IN JAMAICA, IN SEVERAL CARIBBEAN ISLANDS AND IN THE BOARDROOMS OF MANY TOURISM CORPORATIONS THROUGH-OUT THE WORLD. HE BUILT HIS EMPIRE OF ALL-INCLUSIVE HOTELS IN THE CARIBBEAN, STARTING WITH ONE SMALL LOCATION TWENTY-FIVE YEARS AGO. TODAY, SANDALS CONSISTS OF MANY PROPERTIES IN SEVERAL COUNTRIES.

THE SANDALS GROUP IS A REGULAR RECIPIENT OF TOP HONORS AND MAJOR AWARDS IN TOURISM. AS THE DRIVING FORCE BEHIND THE HUGE SUCCESS OF SANDALS, BUTCH STEWART HAS BECOME AN ICON OF ENTREPRENEURIAL SUCCESS IN THE FIELD OF TOURISM EVERYWHERE."

Most Hon. Edward Seaga
Former Prime Minister of Jamaica

4

Growing Strong

SANDALS CREATED A NEW ERA FOR CARIBBEAN TOURISM. THAT SPEAKS VOLUMES ABOUT BUTCH STEWART AND HIS TEAM'S TREMENDOUS VISION AND CONFIDENCE IN THE REGION.

The Hon. Lester Bird
Former Prime Minister of
Antigua and Barbuda

At ten o'clock in the morning on September 12, 1988, Hurricane Gilbert roared furiously toward Morant Point, on the eastern edge of Jamaica. With wind speeds of 130 miles per hour, the strong Category 3 storm bulldozed its way across the entire length of the island, exiting western Jamaica just south of Negril at six o'clock that evening. During its eight-hour rampage, roofs were ripped off buildings, twenty-foot storm surges washed away beachfronts, fierce winds downed trees, and record rainfall flooded roads. Sandals lost nearly its entire hotel inventory within eight hours.

"Every single staff member at Sandals Montego Bay showed up to work the very next day."

CHALLENGING TIMES

"All phone lines were down, it was impossible for us to get through to the hotels from the Kingston office," recalls Stewart's executive assistant, Betty Jo Desnoes. "My husband, John, drove out to the yacht club so he could make his way to a boat and communicate boat-to-boat to find out about the hotels in Montego Bay. He came back with news: total devastation, the last thing we wanted to hear. Mr. Stewart reacted with silence and then began galvanizing. He dispatched every truck he had and bought up every piece of lumber and nails. He called Larry McDonald in and they went through a list of what it would take to get the hotels back in shape. Late that afternoon, we finally got a call through to Miami, where they patched Mr. Stewart through to people all over the world. It was one phone call after another, and Mr. Stewart reassured them that we were fine and that everything would be okay."

Stewart's former wife, P. J., remembers the morning after Gilbert: "The very second that runway was cleared, we took off in the Baron. The damage we witnessed from that small aircraft flying over the north coast was horrendous. Butch was wordless the entire flight. We landed and toured Sandals Montego Bay and Sandals Royal Caribbean; both hotels had been totaled.

STORM SURGE
Hurricane Gilbert leaves behind devastated resorts. Opposite: Travel industry leaders Fred Kassner and Joe Garzilli are impressed by Sandals' phenomenal cleanup efforts after the storm.

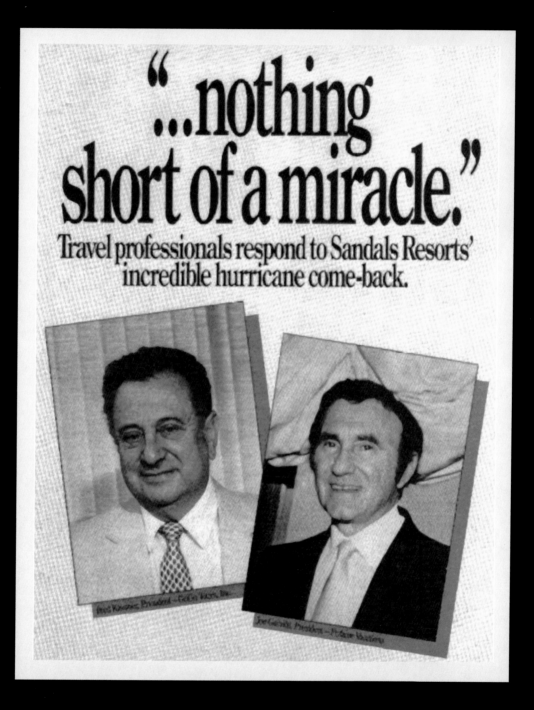

You could sense the wheels spinning in Butch's head, though he was still mostly silent. Then he went into action."

"Every single staff member at Sandals Montego Bay showed up to work the very next day," recalls Merrick Fray, managing director for Sandals Resorts International. "The hotel operator never even went home. She stayed the entire night, through the hurricane. When we saw everyone show up the next morning to get to work, it was the best feeling we ever had. It just made you know that all the hard work, all the interviews were worth it because these were the kinds of people you wanted. And they all came out, every single one of them."

Recalls Sandals Royal Caribbean's general manager at the time, David Roper, who is now group director of industry relations for Sandals Resorts International: "When I came back to the hotel the next morning, you'd not believe it when I tell you that every member of the staff showed up to work. That is incredible, especially considering the amount of personal stuff that they had suffered. I attribute it to total loyalty. Yes, the attitude was that this is where my bread and butter is, but I don't believe it was purely economics. It was a matter of, 'You know, I enjoy what I do. I want to see this thing work.'

Employees knew they could not give up on Jamaica.

"There were waiters moving sand off the lawn. I remember when Mr. Stewart showed up. He saw a devastating sight. They had a meeting at Sandals Montego Bay and got right down to work. Mr. Stewart made a decision: 'Okay, this hotel is least damaged, let's get Sandals Montego Bay up and running first.' He had a plan and mobilized every engineer and technician."

Along with Sandals Montego Bay and Sandals Royal Caribbean, Carlyle on the Bay was also affected. So were the soon-to-open Sandals Negril and Sandals Ocho Rios. The work required in putting the pieces back together of five broken resorts was daunting. With a refuse-to-be-beaten outlook, here again, the spirited Sandals team, along with members of the Appliance Traders Limited staff, rallied together and labored around the clock, tackling the enormous task of refurbishment and reconstruction.

Your Travel Partner

Each year, more than twenty-five thousand guests purchase a Trip Mate Travel Protection Plan designed exclusively for the guests of Sandals and Beaches resorts.

Trip Mate is a leading provider of travel protection plans, insuring millions of vacationers each year. The plans protect guests in the event that they must cancel their vacation, return home early, incur medical expenses, or need assistance during their vacation. Trip Mate also covers damage to or delay of baggage and personal possessions.

"We are proud of our long association with Sandals and Beaches and of our ability to supplement the vacation experience with our quality products and services," says Debra A. McCaffrey, Trip Mate's vice president, client relations. "Our philosophy is simple: Provide the best service possible. We handle claims in a manner that demonstrates our utmost concern for the guest and his or her situation."

"Each and every person at Trip Mate is committed to providing the best service possible."

DEBRA A. MCCAFFREY
VICE PRESIDENT

Trip Mate's claims examiners undergo extensive training and are committed to providing fast, fair and friendly service. Customer service representatives are available around the clock and are always respectful of guest needs and concerns.

Guests do not expect anything to spoil their vacation, but sometimes the unforeseen occurs. When it does, Trip Mate is there, just a phone call away.

Sandals Grande St. Lucian Spa & Beach Resort

Choose Your Destination

Established in 1978, San Jose-based Classic Custom Vacations sells tailored luxury vacations delivering unforgettable experiences. Classic handles all elements of a trip: hotel, air transportation, car rental, special amenities, and tours and activities—all customized together to provide the ideal vacation. By focusing on luxury, Classic has access to the best rooms at the top 4- and 5-star hotels, discounts on first-class and business-class air transportation, and many other options to help travelers feel pampered and well cared for. Available through travel agents as well as through www.classicvacations.com, Classic takes clients on vacations the world over, including to the Caribbean.

"Classic Caribbean is one of the fastest growing of Classic's products. We have focused on very high-end specialized services for travelers," says Ron Letterman, chairman of Classic Custom Vacations. "The Caribbean is a destination where travelers can be as active or as sedentary as they like and where any level of service is available."

Indeed, Sandals and Beaches resorts are Classic's number one partners in the Caribbean. "Sandals and Beaches are ideal for honeymooners and families," says Suzi LeVine, vice president of sales and marketing for Classic. "With everything included, travelers don't have to worry. And, with the training and marketing support Sandals provides, it's easy for travel agents to sell the resorts to their clients."

Classic Custom Vacations sells its product through the best and most knowledgeable travel agents in the United States. "These are people who know our products and our destinations inside and out," says LeVine. "As a result, travelers can rest assured that they're being steered to the best choices for their particular needs and that they'll be delighted with their vacations."

REFIT, RESTORE, REFURBISH

Clever as he was, Stewart knew that an entirely different, yet equally important, restoration was required—that of assuring his valued partners in the travel trade that the resorts would soon be back, and better than ever. Rather than tow the typical industry line, that of minimizing the damage, Stewart took another approach, which was both forthright and forceful. A press conference was hastily arranged.

"Just a few days after Gilbert, Mr. Stewart packs us all up and we head to New York for a press luncheon," says Betty Jo Desnoes. "None of us had electricity or running water in our homes and we just bundled up to go to New York, where we got a hot shower when we arrived!"

At the luncheon, held at Manhattan's Four Seasons Hotel, Stewart initiated a frank and open dialogue with the tour operators and press in attendance. He presented his game plan: Sandals would close the hotels and throw all of its resources into reconstruction and new construction. No Sandals facility would open until it was bigger and better than before. He showed photographs of the devastation as well as the construction progress, which was well under way in just three days. Once again, Stewart assured the apprehensive listeners that everything would be okay in a matter of weeks.

With its credibility on the line, the team had to make a serious commitment to get everything built properly and up to the high standards that the chairman demanded. On a more personal level, every employee, from laborer and groundskeeper, electrician and plumber, to general manager and bellman, knew they could not give up on Jamaica. During this trying time, no one pushed himself harder than Stewart.

"He always set the example in terms of work ethic and never asked you to do something that he would not do himself," says Eleanor Miller, former ATL branch manager and now director of projects for Sandals Resorts International. "He regards the people he works with as his friends. It's very much a family environment. And I think that's why his staff is so committed to him."

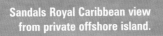
Sandals Royal Caribbean view from private offshore island.

EDYALTHAI

weather report

The forecast for guests traveling to Sandals and Beaches resorts looks good. That's because, in the unlikely event that hurricane-force winds—as defined by the United States National Weather Service—directly hit a Sandals or Beaches resort, interrupting the use of included activities, guests are offered a complimentary replacement holiday, including round-trip airfare. "Guests have nothing to lose, only to gain a replacement holiday," says Butch Stewart.

The Blue Chip Hurricane Guarantee affirms the company's commitment to total customer satisfaction and takes the worry out of booking a Sandals or Beaches vacation any time of the year, including hurricane season. It simply eliminates the risk. "While we do our best to guarantee stress-free and hassle-free vacations at Sandals and Beaches resorts, unfortunately we cannot control the occasional hurricane," says John Lynch, the executive vice president of sales worldwide for Unique Vacations. "With the Blue Chip Hurricane Guarantee, guests can trust the Sandals and Beaches brands to stand behind their pledge to replace all vacations interrupted by a hurricane."

"Mr. Stewart wanted things done a certain way."

TIME TO SHINE

That commitment paid off. Within a month, on October 14, 1988, Sandals Montego Bay reopened. Sandals brought in travel agents and tour operators by the planeloads to ensure that they experienced the "new" resort firsthand, and they were appropriately wined and dined by the Sandals team.

Crunchtime took on new meaning for Sandals as the resorts reopened and new hotels came on line. This was now an opportunity for Sandals to shine, and standards were set very, very high. "After Gilbert, that was the test of the organization," reflects Merrick Fray. "We had to open the new resorts up in quick succession, interview and find managers and staff. It was tough work."

SELLING UP, STRETCHING OUT
Left: Sandals staffers Wayne Swanson, far left, and Betty Jo Desnoes, middle, sell the resorts at an industry trade show. Above: Another perfect day in paradise.

"Even with all the confusion going on with construction, hiring staff, etcetera, Mr. Stewart wanted things done a certain way. He wanted things put a certain way. It had to look spectacular," recalls Eleanor Miller of that hectic time. "He has an eye for detail and sees color and style in a way that a lot of people don't see. When he walks onto a property for an inspection, the standards better apply, because nothing passes by him, make no bones about it. I clearly remember one evening two weeks before Sandals Negril opened. Mr. Stewart called a meeting at nine o'clock that evening. Finally, at one o'clock in the morning, he decided to do a site walk with us, the bleary-eyed staff, trailing behind him. He stopped at the bar by the pool and snapped at Evan, the architect, 'What is that?' Evan said, 'That's the pool bar.' Mr. Stewart said, 'No, you've got to be joking. It's much too small. Take it down.' I thought the construction people were going to have a heart attack! Guess what? It got knocked down, and they put up what was required—a larger pool bar. It didn't matter that it was two weeks before the opening."

The construction crew may have been cranky, but the Sandals Negril Grand Opening party that November was a huge celebration. By the next morning, though, it was back to work. Sandals Royal Caribbean needed to open shortly thereafter and it did, on December 12, 1988, exactly three months after Hurricane Gilbert.

"Everything was open and up and running by Christmas," recalls former Flyfaire tour operator Warren Cohen, now senior vice president of marketing and sales development for Unique Vacations. "I remember that the product showed an incredible change. It was much better. I think it was just evolution—Sandals rebuilt based on its hotel experience during the past seven years. The hurricane destroyed everything and, since they were basically starting from scratch, they built the hotels more in mind with their vision of how the hotels should be."

COME AGAIN
Travel agents and guests arrive one month after Hurricane Gilbert at the newly reopened Sandals Montego Bay.

Pickering photo

THE REOPENING of the all-inclusive Sandals Montego Bay hotel over the weekend, after being closed by Hurricane Gilbert on September 12, was celebrated with a grand beach party around the hotel's Pool Bar on Sunday. Thirty Sunburst travel agents were flown in from the United States of America just for the day to see for themselves "that we are ready" said General Manager, Ewart McKie. They, along with other travel agents who had arrived on Saturday and just under 100 guests, were treated to an evening of wining, dining and beach frolic. Here Mr. McKie (4th from right) join Entertainment Manager, Paul Tomlinson and Playmakers in welcoming the travel agents to the hotel.

Adler Insurance Group

Team Support

Team members at Unique Vacations, the worldwide representatives for Sandals and Beaches resorts, enjoy many benefits. "Unique Vacations provides quality insurance for its staff and, in return, gains loyal and caring employees," says Robert Adler, president of Adler Insurance Group, which has provided the employee benefit plans for many years.

"I have insured many businesses and individuals, from international entertainers to dolphin research facilities," adds Adler. "What makes Unique Vacations different is that it operates as one family. It's rare to find that kind of quality in today's business environment."

"As their insurance agent, I have gotten to know the executives, managers and employees personally. We have helped many team members and their families obtain critical care. But by far, my greatest satisfaction comes when I assist them in getting employees well and back to work, and seeing the company take care of its own during tough times."

Butch Stewart and Robert Adler

Sandals kept looking for ways to make the all-inclusive vacation experience better. By this time, there were at least two specialty restaurants at each resort. More Jacuzzis and gazebos were placed around the properties. Furnishings were upgraded. Bathrooms started to be tiled right up to the ceiling, and the overall quality was vastly improved.

Stewart took an interest in the beds at this point and wanted only the very best mattresses. As the number of resorts increased dramatically, everything was methodically planned and positioned. Now there were three properties in Montego Bay, one resort in Negril and a new Sandals resort opening on the north coast—Sandals Ocho Rios.

Stewart had promoted a very young hotel manager, Horace Peterkin, to the position of general manager at the new Sandals Ocho Rios. Peterkin recalls: "One day Mr. Stewart came to see me when I was the general manager of the Carlyle and said, 'Listen young fellow, you know we have this new hotel in Ocho Rios and I think you're ready to take it on. How do you feel about it?' I replied, 'Are you serious? Wow! Yes I'm ready.' But I was cautiously optimistic because

OCHO RIOS OPENING
Above: Sandals Ocho Rios being built. Left: Former Jamaica Prime Minister the Right Honorable Michael Manley chats with Butch Stewart during the Grand Opening of the new resort, seen below.

when you move from a 52-room hotel to a 237-room hotel, it is a lot more responsibility. It was a huge leap."

Peterkin made the leap in grand style and he proved to be the perfect fit for the impressive new resort, which opened with four specialty restaurants, hundreds of tropical plants and gardens—from fruit trees to herbal plants and orchids—and ponds filled with carp, perch and goldfish. Buildings displayed a Mediterranean architecture, so it was no wonder that the hotel was dubbed the "Caribbean Riviera."

It was during a ceremony at the Grand Opening of Sandals Ocho Rios, on April 15, 1989, that Stewart first publicly announced that the Sandals group would "go Caribbean." He stated that he was committed to making the Sandals hotel chain a Caribbean resort company. "When you spread into the Caribbean, you get market clout," he said.

But before island-hopping, Sandals would open one more Jamaican resort in Ocho Rios. It would be the *pièce de résistance*: Sandals Dunn's River.

THE BUS WON'T HOLD THEM BACK: Two staff members of Sandals Montego Bay (hotel) are set to go on new motorcycles bought under a revolving loan fund established by the hotel to help staff overcome transport problems. Under the scheme, the hotel has puts all the funds for the purchase and even licensing of the motorcycles and staff pay back at very minimal interest rates, said Horace Peterkin (centre) general manager. The two staff members here, Glaister Pennicott (left) and Christopher Lannaman of the Dining Room, are expected to get to work and increase their productivity now that they won't be able to say: "The bus was late."

START YOUR ENGINES
Sandals staff members, always on the go, pictured with General Manager Horace Peterkin, middle.

Edward Don & Company

Well-Equipped

Did you know that today Sandals operates more than one hundred and fifty restaurants? One of the secrets to the restaurants' success is an efficient behind-the-scenes operation. "With a setup like ours, we've got to rely on excellent food-service suppliers," says Armando Pizutti, Sandals group director of food and beverage.

For nearly two decades, Edward Don & Company, the leading distributor of food-service equipment and supplies in the United States, has outfitted Sandals with everything for the kitchen and table—from fine china, flatware and glassware to ovens, ranges and refrigerators. "We're a family-owned business that has been in operation since 1921," says Steve Don, the company's president and CEO. "And we would like other families to benefit from our services."

"It's a pleasure to work with Sandals. Like them, we're dedicated to delivering top-notch service."

STEVE DON
PRESIDENT AND CEO

The Mark Travel Corporation commends Butch Stewart for his many examples of commitment to excellence, not just for Sandals but for the people and island of Jamaica.

Making Its

Butch Stewart, chairman of Sandals Resorts, gets an earful when he calls Bill La Macchia, chief executive officer of The Mark Travel Corporation. The earful, however, is spoken with admiration and respect. La Macchia refers to Stewart as "the entrepreneur's hero." So when Stewart calls, La Macchia always answers with "Butch, my hero."

In the early 1980s, La Macchia met Stewart on the patio of a resort in Ocho Rios. At that time, Stewart had just acquired two resorts, but it was obvious his dream would not stop there. During that short meeting it became apparent to La Macchia that he was in the presence of a true visionary.

Mark

The Mark Travel Corporation has been creating memorable vacation dreams and experiences for a multitude of vacationers each year since 1974. The travel company was launched when owner and president William E. La Macchia envisioned a vacation company focusing on the needs of travel agents and vacationers. He began his company as Funway Holidays, established The Mark Travel Corporation in 1983, and has gradually consolidated seventeen vacation companies under this corporate umbrella.

The Mark Travel Corporation commends Butch Stewart for his many examples of commitment to excellence, not just for Sandals but for the people and island of Jamaica. One example, which was a personal experience for The Mark Travel Corporation and Funjet Vacations, occurred in 1988 just after Hurricane Gilbert hit Jamaica. The island had suffered greatly after the storm and was in the midst of being brought back into shape. Butch Stewart and Bill La Macchia decided to sponsor a one-day trip to the island for travel agents from the Midwest to show them that Jamaica was ready to handle tourists. Stewart made sure that the agents toured all around Jamaica, not just spending their time at Sandals. Stewart's commitment to the island and its people was apparent, says La Macchia.

For The Mark Travel Corporation and its customers, Sandals and Beaches resorts remain a "hot" destination. "The Sandals team has a knack for attracting thousands of visitors to its resorts, yet making them feel exclusively a visitor's own," says La Macchia. "That's how a Sandals visit transcends simply 'being away' and becomes a memorable vacation experience. This has always been a hallmark of Sandals' success and we are thrilled to be a part of it."

Tom Meier, executive vice president of The Mark Travel Corporation, recalls Stewart's vision: "I remember one time when I flew on a private plane with the Sandals team to Negril. Butch showed me his plans for the new resort, but at the time all I could see were palm trees and a beach! As we drank coconut milk while sitting by the beach, Butch explained the new resort in exacting detail with such pride and joy. I thought, well, here's a real visionary and someone with a true passion for the travel industry."

Shortly after, when the Sandals dream became reality and Funjet Vacations, the flagship brand of The Mark Travel Corporation, started marketing Jamaica aggressively, Funjet knew that in order to succeed in Jamaica, it needed to have a relationship with Sandals Resorts. The two companies got together and forged a strong bond that continues to this day.

Bill La Macchia, left, and Butch Stewart

WATER WORLD
Sandals Dunn's River, pictured at right, opens with a splash in 1991. At the time, the resort boasts the Caribbean's largest swimming pool.

EVERYBODY IN THE POOL!

Xayamaca, or land of wood and water, was the name that the Arawak Indians called Jamaica when they first inhabited the island in about A.D. 650. Surely they were inspired by the island's magnificent waterfalls, Dunn's River Falls among them.

Dunn's River Falls is a living, growing marvel. The 600-foot waterfall continually renews itself from deposits of travertine rock, the result of the precipitation of calcium carbonate from the river as it flows over the falls. Each year, visitors by the thousands flock to Ocho Rios, where the Falls are located, to trek along the most-talked-about Jamaican attraction. Butch Stewart and his creative team must have also been inspired by the Falls, when, in 1990, they started a massive refurbishment of the property.

"We blew everyone away and gave them a

huge water playground and they loved it."

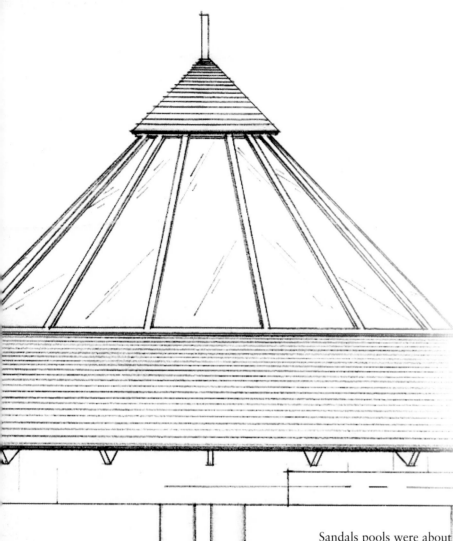

"We gutted the place and spent twice as much fixing it up as we had bought it for," boasted Stewart at the time. "Sandals Dunn's River is going to be spectacular; it will be the resort of its era. It's a creative time; we want to stay way ahead of the competition, and we're just going to do giant things and stay way ahead."

They stayed way ahead by constructing a replica of Dunn's River Falls right on the property, surrounded by the Caribbean's largest swimming pool ever.

"At first we were a little hesitant to build a replica of Dunn's River, but it certainly worked," recalls architect Evan Williams. "Hey, ten thousand square feet of water has got to impress, and that pool became a highlight of the property. We knew from past history that our guests didn't want to just swim in the pools; they wanted to wade in them, to hang out and party in them. All Sandals pools were about five feet deep. But the pool at Sandals Dunn's River really was an innovation and a way for us to give the guests more of what they wanted rather than use the old standard. We blew everyone away and gave them a huge water playground and they loved it."

The pool may have been the focal point, but there were several other innovations to brag about: dramatic architecture, luxurious rooms and suites, and excellent staff and service.

TOUR DE FORCE
Below: Former Jamaica Prime Minister the Right Honorable Michael Manley, far left, and GOGO Worldwide Vacations co-founder Fred Kassner, second from left, tour the new Sandals Dunn's River with executives of Unique Vacations.

"BY THE EARLY 1990s, SANDALS RESORTS HAD BECOME A MAJOR FORCE IN THE TRAVEL INDUSTRY. WITH STEWART AT THE HELM, THE COMPANY CONTINUED TO PUSH THE ENVELOPE AND FINE-TUNE ITS HOTEL PRODUCT. GUESTS WERE OFFERED MORE CHOICES WITH A GREATER RANGE OF SERVICES, AMENITIES AND DESTINATIONS. CONSUMERS WERE NOW WALKING INTO TRAVEL AGENCIES AND ASKING TO GO TO SANDALS. WE WERE A DESTINATION AND A RECOGNIZED BRAND."

Mandy Chomat
Senior Vice President, Sales and Marketing
Unique Vacations, Inc.

"I had worked on property at Sandals Montego Bay, Sandals Royal Caribbean and Sandals Negril," recalls former rooms-division manager Wayne Cummings, now a general manager with Sandals. "I thought Sandals Dunn's River was going to be Mr. Stewart's opportunity to put a prime marble-and-brass product out there. That was my interpretation and it was coming true because here was this massive pool. I couldn't imagine anybody spending money to put fifty seats at a pool bar, but it was looking fabulous. Our pool tile designer, Val Carol, created this fantastic pool design. She did all the waves and designs you see in the pool by hand. I remember her in that pool tiling at midnight. Everybody who was participating on that job, from architects to painters to subcontractors to staff, was thrilled and excited and knew they were creating something very special."

The property has an interesting history. It originated as the Arawak Hotel in 1958; became a Hilton Hotel in the early 1960s; segued into the Americana; and then transformed into Eden II in the early 1970s. Eden II was the first and only hotel that famed architect Morris Lapidus designed in Jamaica. Lapidus, renowned for Miami Beach's glamorous Fountainbleau and Eden Roc hotels, also brought his distinctive style to Eden II.

"I called his son, who's an architect, and he lent me the original hotel drawings," recounts Evan Williams. "They were inspiring in their own right and served as a catalyst for us to create our own imagery."

OUTDOOR DINING
Above: Guests enjoy a gourmet meal poolside. Below: A newspaper advertisement touts a new resort.

Leaders in Travel

For fifty-seven years, Garber Travel, ranked as the fourteenth-largest travel agency in the United States, has distinguished itself as a leader in vacations and corporate travel management by providing clients with unparalleled service and exceptional value. The company's commitment, flexibility and years of time-tested experience set it apart in an ever-changing industry. As the largest independently owned agency headquartered in New England, Garber Travel operates more than eighty locations in the United States, London and Toronto.

Roz Garber, president of Garber Travel, and her late husband, Lou, spent a number of memorable vacations at Sandals. "I recall our first trip to Sandals Montego Bay in June 1983," says Roz Garber. "Lou and I were seated with a number of other couples and were discussing the new property and the Sandals concept. One of those seated at the table was none other than Butch Stewart. We were delighted to meet him and were impressed by his enthusiasm and vision. Lou returned to Boston raving about the vacation experience and we immediately added Sandals to our preferred supplier list."

Lou and Roz Garber enjoy their first trip to Sandals, June 1983

Caribbean travel and honeymoon planning are two of Garber Travel's specialties, so Sandals was a great fit. And, like Sandals, Garber Travel built its organization on the principle that "service is key" when it comes to customer satisfaction. The company has a total commitment to providing excellent service to clients. It accomplishes this goal by focusing on client needs and managing the agency's own business efficiently, utilizing innovative technology and recognizing the contributions of a skilled and dedicated staff.

Garber Travel has distinguished itself as a leader in vacations and corporate travel management.

Top photo: Sandals Resorts International

A postcard of Sandals Dunn's River, pictured at right, is reminiscent of Italy's Lake Como, another of the resort's inspirations.

The image that emerged was based on Italy's Lake Como. "Many of the hotel's touches were inspired by Italian influences," continues Williams. "In Lake Como, it's common to see magnificent high-rises by the sea. That entry, as you drive down, is reminiscent of the ones at hotels in and around northern Italy. Every time a new Sandals property opens, something innovative takes place, which enhances what came before."

Well-regarded Sandals Dunn's River hotel General Manager Louis Grant oversaw the property details and insisted on having the best staff, from housekeeping to rooms division to entertainment. He knew this resort was going to be the showpiece. "We made new benchmarks for the company with Sandals Dunn's River," beams Grant, "and everything was set to incredibly high standards and great expectations. With the experience of our other hotels, we were now able to put everything in place. Sandals Dunn's River incorporated the best assets of the other Sandals properties at the time."

Heave-Ho Charters

Out to Sea

Captain P.J. Gibson sounded a conch shell announcing the arrival of the Heave-Ho schooner to Sandals Ocho Rios on April 18, 1989. "Our first guests were greeted with our company motto, 'You're not here for a long time, so let's make it a good time,'" recalls Gibson.

In the early 1990s, Heave-Ho Cruises participated in Sandals' weekly beach parties. "What a spectacular sight when floodlights lit the dark seas to find our fifty-four-foot schooner under full sails," he adds.

Today, Heave-Ho Charters boasts a fleet of five, providing cruises for all Sandals and Beaches properties in Ocho Rios. Party-seekers can hop aboard *Cool Jazz*, a sixty-foot fast Cat, regarded as the area's premier party vessel. Or, for those who yearn for a relaxed day with champagne cocktails, Heave-Ho offers the thirty-nine-foot Jeanot Privilege luxury yacht, *Sapphire Cat*.

OPERATION VACATION

Just as the finishing touches were being placed around the resort in preparation for its opening, dramatic events were taking place around the world. On January 16, 1991, United States President George H.W. Bush launched Desert Storm with massive air and missile attacks on Iraq and Kuwait.

Wanting to show appreciation to the American-led allied forces, Sandals gave the best way it could—by offering $1 million in weeklong vacations to Gulf War military personnel.

Stewart explains, "We feel that Sandals had a mission in the Persian Gulf conflict, too, one of tangible support. We knew that when the men and women returned from action they would welcome the opportunity to retreat to the Caribbean for a relaxing vacation."

Relatives of the armed forces read about the promotion, dubbed "Operation Sandals," in *USA Today, The Washington Post, The Los Angeles Times, The Wall Street Journal* and the *New York Daily News*, among other newspapers. They were encouraged to send in postcards with names and details of soldiers.

"We received more than 250 postcards per day from husbands, wives, relatives and friends of those serving in the conflict," says Stewart.

On February 27, President Bush declared Kuwait as liberated and suspended offensive combat. Within the next few months, thousands of coalition forces returned home. Five hundred of them were selected in a sweepstake drawing and headed off to Sandals for some well-deserved rest and relaxation.

The opening of Sandals Dunn's River stands as a milestone in the history of Sandals resorts. With the opening, Sandals became the largest operator of fully all-inclusive resorts in the Caribbean and Jamaica's second-largest employer. (The Jamaican government was number one.)

The range of choices for guests was unprecedented. It was now "Stay at One, Play at Six" in Jamaica.

The phenomenon of Sandals was taking off.

STAFF Sgt. Daniel Stamaris, the U.S. Army crew chief and celebrated POW, drew the first of 500 winning names in a $1 million Sandals vacation sweepstakes for Persian Gulf vets. Lucky servicepersons will receive week-long sojourns for two at Sandals Resorts in Jamaica. Stamaris was one of three survivors in a dramatic helicopter re mission during Operation Desert Shield. Sandals VP of Marketing Development Warren Cohen and Rene Stamaris (wife) assisted.

US 'Operations Desert Storm' troops get free vacations

TROOP TRIBUTE

A United States staff sergeant, center, gratefully accepts one of the weeklong Sandals vacations provided by Unique Vacations from its vice president, Warren Cohen. Sandals donated $1 million worth of trips to Gulf War military personnel in 1991.

STAY AT ONE, PLAY AT SIX.

By now Sandals was regarded as a resort group that had perfected the all-inclusive vacation, and it was time to spread Sandals' wings over a second fabulous Caribbean destination.

But, which would be right for Sandals?

Antigua

All things considered—political stability, warm and friendly people, and good airlift—the island of Antigua looked extremely appealing.

BOSS AT THE BEACH
In his signature blue-stripe shirt, Butch Stewart surveys his new resort, Sandals Antigua, whose beach is pictured at right.

When the opportunity arose to buy the ninety-nine-room Divi Resort, a low-rise property sprawled across twelve acres like a Caribbean village, Sandals took it. For well-known beach-connoisseur Butch Stewart, the crescent-shaped powdered sand beach of Dickenson Bay was among the Caribbean's best.

"Mr. Stewart loves the Caribbean, and the beach is what fascinates him," says Merrick Fray. "Whenever he sends any of us to scout a property, the first thing he inquires about is the beach and the sand. Next he asks, 'How was the swimming?' You have to go into the water, swim, and let him know how it was. I recall one time when I actually carried back a sample of sand in a little jar. I handed him the jar and said, 'See, this is what it looks like.'"

With 365 beaches, one for each day of the year, the island of Antigua was sure to be a success with Sandals' guests. After acquiring the property, the team went to work refurbishing and expanding the resort to bring it up to the Sandals standard.

Sandals made its mark on the island of Antigua, bringing forth a level of professionalism and quality of product that left a lasting impression with the local tourism industry. Dr. Rodney Williams, then Antigua's minister of tourism, worked closely with the Sandals team to help promote the new all-inclusive resort and the island.

"Antigua was fortunate to be the first destination outside of Jamaica to benefit from having Sandals' presence," says Williams. "Whereas formerly many hotels were run by non-Caribbean people, here came an up-market hotel chain run by local Caribbeans that delivered a high quality of service.

The Hon. Lester Bird, former prime minister of Antigua and Barbuda, concurs. "Sandals created a new era for Caribbean tourism," he says. "That speaks volumes about Butch Stewart and his team's tremendous vision and confidence in the region."

"Mr. Stewart loves the Caribbean, and the beach is what fascinates him."

The Week in Travel

Travelweek, Canada's best read travel trade publication, has been providing industry news and destination information to thirteen thousand travel agents and to other industry personnel across the country for the past thirty years. In addition to its weekly magazine, *Travelweek* also publishes travel agent manuals covering destinations in Europe, Canada and the Caribbean, plus *The Blue Book*, an annual industry directory. *Travelweek* is also the driving force behind the Toronto Travel & Leisure Show, a biannual event that attracts over twenty thousand consumers and more than fifteen hundred travel professionals.

For more than ten years, *Travelweek* has been helping to keep Canadian travel agents informed and up-to-date about Sandals and Beaches resorts. "Sandals is the first word in all-inclusive sun vacations and, for some travelers, the only word," says *Travelweek* publisher Gerry Kinasz. "Our writers have visited the Sandals properties and kept our readers abreast of all the latest news. We've also helped spread the word about Sandals company events and promotions, and educated readers about the Certified Sandals Specialist program."

Indeed, *Travelweek* maintains a strong partnership with Sandals. "Canada is one of our top international markets," says Gary Sadler, director of sales and marketing for Unique Vacations in Canada. "The publication has worked hard to contribute to our success in the region."

Travelweek has also joined with Sandals on The YellowBird Foundation, a charitable organization dedicated to community development at Canada's favorite travel destinations. A key focus of The YellowBird Foundation is improving the lives of children in the Caribbean and Latin America by supporting local education and school programs.

> *"Sandals is a results-oriented company with a fantastic track record for providing the ultimate in upscale all-inclusive vacations."*
>
> GERRY KINASZ
> PUBLISHER

MEET AND GREET
Above: Stewart, second from right, shakes hands with Horace Peterkin, the general manager who opened the new Antigua resort.

One of the great successes of Sandals Antigua is the remarkable integration of staff and service that took place. At the time, Sandals was regarded as a Jamaican organization. Before it could simply run a resort on another island it had to properly ingratiate itself. And, how was that accomplished?

"The people we brought over to do training showed genuine concern," says Wayne Cummings, who was rooms division manager at the time. "We showed them that we treated staff as family and were a good company to work for, and we proved it over and over again—by talking about Mr. Stewart and his philosophy, and by sending them to Jamaica. We made sure they had an opportunity to come to Jamaica to share this whole experience. I was proud of that. I was proud to be able to stand tall and talk about the culture and say this is why we're successful. And it became a part of their culture."

Quaint, charismatic and very romantic, Sandals Antigua went on to become a property especially beloved by honeymooners. The resort was also a steppingstone from which Sandals would stride as it went on to open several more resorts on exotic Caribbean islands. The wings had spread.

A
Sandals
RESORT

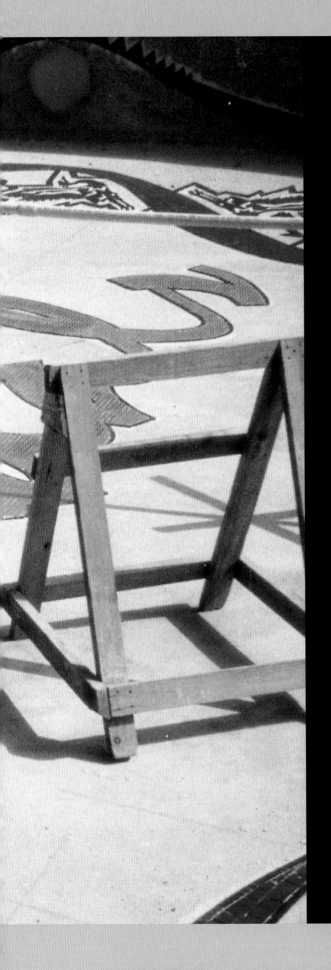

5

Building
A Brand

YOU CANNOT HAVE A STRONG BRAND
UNLESS YOU HAVE A STRONG PRODUCT.
SANDALS HAS BUILT AND DELIVERED
AN EVER-IMPROVING, EVER-EVOLVING,
VERY DYNAMIC PRODUCT, WHICH MEANS
THAT OUR BRANDING HAS ALSO BEEN
ABLE TO EVOLVE. TODAY SANDALS IS A
GLOBALLY RECOGNIZED NAME.

Tony Cortizas
Director of Advertising
Unique Vacations

ON DISPLAY

New York-based sales manager Maura Cecere's phone rang one day in late October 1991. Butch Stewart was on the other end. "Maura," he shouted. "You know these new stand-up displays we've just printed?" "Yes," answered Cecere. She and the rest of the sales team had viewed the dramatic six-foot-high, four-color, cube-like displays at a recent sales meeting. "Good. I want you to get them set up in one thousand travel agencies . . . before Christmas! Just do whatever you have to and get it done."

"I thought to myself, wow, here we are in the throes of a recession with everyone cutting back on advertising dollars, except us," reflects Cecere. "But Butch Stewart has always marched to the beat of his own drum."

While proud to work for an organization that was committed to supporting travel agents with training, collateral and now displays, Cecere took note of her calendar and, for a minute, was daunted by the task. With the hectic holiday season around the corner, not to mention her own wedding in November, she wondered how she would get the displays shipped and assembled in one thousand agencies in time. But if ever there was a can-do sales manager, it was Cecere. "I hired housewives, college kids, whomever I could find to get those displays into their cars and set up at agencies throughout New York, New Jersey and Connecticut."

In typical fashion, Sandals blanketed the market with its colorful, distinctive brand of advertising. The dynamic new displays were in nearly every agency window throughout the Northeast.

"We go all out," says Stewart, "so that word-of-mouth becomes a powerful and permanent promotional plus."

"When we created the **first consumer brochure,** what we wanted to do was **capture the feel** of this place."

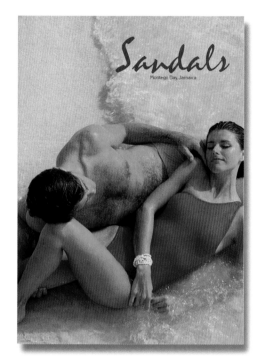

BRANDING IN THE BEGINNING

Ever evolving, ever innovative, ever effective. The Sandals brand is one of the most recognized in the travel industry. It started with a simple visual—a couple sitting on the sand, the woman concealed by her wide-brimmed hat. Through the years, Sandals advertising and marketing has developed into a sophisticated, colorful worldwide campaign.

Sandals has always taken a novel approach to branding, starting with the very first brochure and advertising campaign designed by Adrian Robinson in 1981.

"Essentially, when we created the first consumer brochure, what we wanted to do was capture the feel of this place, which was quite unique in the way that the services were delivered," recalls Robinson. "The photography style evoked a true Caribbean ambience, the feeling of relaxation and being at the beach. It was a way of seeing a Jamaican hotel that was different from what everyone else was doing at the time. Right from the start, the notion was to feature the resort concept and the service."

Twenty-plus years later, the resort concept and the service remain the cornerstones of the brand.

Sandals

RESORT BEACH CLUB
Montego Bay, Jamaica

Beaches® Family Resort By Sandals

Every piece of collateral
is equivalent to a
drop of Caribbean
sunshine that's
landed on a page.

ROMANCING THE RESORT

Though bricks and mortar, Sandals truly is a
concept—a vacation experience that is a romantic
couples-only escape to the Caribbean, one of the
world's most exotic destinations. The whole notion
of romance, couples and spending quality time
together is an ongoing lifestyle theme that runs
throughout all the branding materials. "We represent that feel-good, in-love sentiment that everyone
wants," Unique Vacations director of advertising Tony
Cortizas points out. "Everyone craves a successful romantic
life, and Sandals has always tapped directly into that
emotion and pulled that heartstring."

COLORFUL COLLATERAL
**As the number of Sandals and Beaches resorts
grew, so did the amazing array of collateral.
Specially designed property-specific photo
albums and brochures capture the fun and
fantasy of these Caribbean getaways.**

Certainly the Sandals imagery
remains distinctive. An enthusiasm and
vitality appears on every page, billboard and brochure, enlivened by a profu-
sion of images and eye-popping color. "I refer to every piece of collateral as
being equivalent to a drop of Caribbean sunshine that's landed on a page,"
says Cortizas. "If you stand on the shore in the Caribbean and you turn 360
degrees and take your sunglasses off, the white-sand beach is dazzling, the
blue waters are overwhelming, and the greens of the palm trees and colors of
the flowers are hypnotic."

Not only does the landscape command attention, but also the all-
inclusive nature of Sandals itself demands visualization. "We offer such a
high level of quality in terms of accommodations, food, and land and water
sports that one image can't capture everything you want to show," says
Cortizas. "Simply put, Sandals has a product worth displaying, therefore
we're proud to show it off."

Tying The Knot

In 1996, the world of wedding and honeymoon planning fundamentally changed when The Knot launched the world's first online wedding resource. Sandals, always a marketing innovator, recognized the opportunity to reach out to honeymooners on the Web and launched its first online advertising campaign on The Knot.

The Knot, the most comprehensive wedding resource, was founded to offer a sophisticated, easy-to-use and up-to-date alternative to traditional bridal magazines. The Knot quickly became America's leading wedding brand, reaching millions of engaged couples through its award-winning Web site, magazines, books, and content partnerships with AOL, Yahoo! and MSN. The signature fresh voice and powerful interactive tools provide a welcome relief to the stresses of wedding planning.

Well over two million visitors trust TheKnot.com for wedding-planning solutions. The site provides down-to-earth editorial, endless photo galleries, local listings, a honeymoon directory, online shopping, a gift registry, interactive planning tools, and the largest online gallery of wedding gowns.

TheKnot.com revolutionized the wedding-planning process.

The Knot applies its knowledge of bridal consumers to create innovative publications and programs that benefit both brides and the resources interested in reaching them. *The Knot Weddings*, a best-selling magazine, replaced traditional advertisements with alphabetized guides to everything bridal. The magazine's travel directory works with The Knot Honeymoon Search so couples can browse hundreds of resorts. Year after year, Sandals Resorts ranks as the "most-searched" honeymoon retailer on TheKnot.com, receiving more than 1.4 million impressions in 2003 alone.

"We've gone into every nook and cranny that we can find as a way to build brand," continues Tony Cortizas. "From billboards to newspapers, magazines, niche markets like bridal books, and television. Our partnership marketing programs with tour operators and travel agents are aggressive. We run extensive co-op advertising and local guerrilla marketing with travel agents, working hard to develop local promotional programs with them.

"The same applies to the collateral that we develop. The material addresses every phase of purchasing a leisure product, from consumer brochures to informative brochures for agents. We hit them with faxes, e-mails and flyers and were one of the first travel companies to develop very dynamic point-of-purchase display materials, including poster programs and large stand-up displays for agency windows. Our aim is to immerse consumers into the Sandals experience before they even dip their toes into tropical waters."

Islands Media

Isles Aplenty

When consumers want to know the leading islands to travel to, they pick up an issue of *ISLANDS* magazine and dream about faraway destinations. The magazine covers everything from beaches and nightlife to "can't miss" attractions and "hot deals."

"We've evolved from one title published six times per year to four titles published seventeen times per year, thanks to the support of Sandals and other blue-chip advertisers," says ISLANDS Media publisher William J. Kasch. "It's been a pleasure representing the Sandals and Beaches resorts in our magazines and online properties, and enjoying the positive responses from our readers."

ISLANDS Media publishes *ISLANDS*, *SPA*, *ISLANDS Weddings & Honeymoons*, and *Resorts & Great Hotels*. More than one million readers explore their pages in search of their next perfect getaway.

"The Sandals product is a testimony of what vision, dedication and hard work will do for a brand, destination and industry."

WILLIAM J. KASCH
PUBLISHER

"We make it easy for consumers to connect with our brands."

SPIN CYCLE

A power-packed publicity and promotions team complements Sandals' strong advertising campaigns. "We have one of the most innovative publicity and promotion departments in the industry," says John Lynch, Unique Vacations executive vice president of sales worldwide.

With on-property musical concerts by *NSYNC, celebrity sports events including tennis marvel Pete Sampras and Hollywood stars like Carmen Electra, Jessica Simpson and Nick Lachey, and with national promotions with Microsoft® XBOX and Toys "R" Us, it's easy to see how Sandals and Beaches resorts have become household names.

"We try to reach customers in their everyday lives," says Maggie Rivera, Unique Vacations director of public relations and sales promotions. "As media becomes increasingly niched, it is important that our brands and their message impact our target audience in the places that are meaningful to them. For Beaches, that means reaching parents through the traditional parenting publications and in the places they shop, like Toys "R" Us. We make it easy for consumers to connect with our brands."

STAR GAZING
Far left: Hollywood celebrities and real-life lovebirds Jessica Simpson and Nick Lachey at the celebrity Golf Classic. Above: Elmo poses with Butch Stewart. Left: *NSYNC belts out pop tunes at a celebrity concert held at Beaches Turks & Caicos Resort & Spa.

Another impressive promotional program includes a multi-year partnership between Beaches Resorts and Sesame Workshop, the nonprofit educational organization behind *Sesame Street*® and other innovative products and programs for children. "This program literally brings *Sesame Street* to Beaches resorts for daily appearances by characters, including Elmo, Zoe, Cookie Monster and Grover, to educate and entertain young families," says Rivera. "We have on-site year-round *Sesame Street*-themed events, including character dining, special story times, parenting seminars, and a host of other activities. Beaches is committed to providing vacations where families can thoroughly enjoy their time together."

"We are associated with high quality and value for money. Our promotional partners must also represent those values."

PUBLICITY MACHINE

The power of Sandals' and Beaches' promotions and celebrity events carries far and wide. The company has launched many successful promotions, both on property and off, with top-name strategic partners, including television, radio and print outlets. On the small screen, the company has run promotions with Nickelodeon and its *Blue's Clues* program, ABC Family and the Cartoon Network. Other media outlets that the company has regularly worked with include *Redbook* and all the major bridal publications, such as *Brides, Modern Bride, Bridal Guide*, Weddingchannel.com and *The Knot*, among many others. For over a decade, Sandals has also conducted local and national radio promotions in conjunction with radio giant Clear Channel Communications.

"When it comes to our promotions, we are very careful about aligning ourselves with the right strategic partners," says Rivera. "Sandals and Beaches resorts has worked diligently to develop a strong image in the marketplace. We are associated with high quality and value for money. Our promotional partners must also represent those values."

Beaches has also teamed up with Microsoft to create the first Microsoft® XBOX Game Oasis video game centers in the Caribbean. Today, kids and adults vacationing at Beaches are thrilled when they find the resort outfitted with the hottest game titles and top gaming system. Promotional partnerships for the Sandals WeddingMoons and Beaches FamilyMoons programs include the premier wedding accessories designer Beverly Clark, celebrity wedding designer and planner Preston Bailey, and leading luxury home collections group Waterford Wedgwood.

ON THE SCENE AT SANDALS
Top left: Actress Melissa Joan Hart is flanked by Justin Timberlake, left, and Chris Kirkpatrick. Bottom left: Comedian Kathy Griffin is flanked by Jaime-Lynn DiScala, left, and musician Lance Bass. Top: Larger-than-life sports star Michael Jordan. Right: *The Sopranos'* stars and Paul Sorvino, second from right, gather at a celebrity event. Far right: Carmen Electra sizzles at Sandals.

Honeymoon Helpers

Sandals first catered to brides and grooms with the opening of Sandals Montego Bay in 1981. Ever since, the Sandals team has developed innovative programs to make the matrimony experience—and honeymoon—even more memorable.

In October 2002, Sandals formed the first-ever online honeymoon registry with WeddingChannel.com, the leading source for engaged couples seeking guidance on the world of weddings and honeymoons. This interactive Web site is aimed at future brides and grooms and their wedding guests. Couples have fun planning their dream wedding with WeddingChannel.com's comprehensive suite of content and tools. There are more than thirty thousand photographs, articles and pieces of advice on everything about weddings: from gowns and flowers to cakes and honeymoon hot spots.

Wedding guests can easily search for a couple's registry to find the ideal gift.

With over 1.5 million registries in its database, WeddingChannel.com offers the family and friends of the betrothed an easy one-stop-shop for gifts the couples most desire.

"The idea to take registry one step further was based on the growing trend of brides and grooms who get married later in life and who want non-traditional registries. "This partnership provides couples with the opportunity to expand their registry choices from conventional home goods to more modern ideas like honeymoon registries," says Mandy Chomat, senior vice president of sales and marketing for Unique Vacations.

Brides and grooms who book a Sandals honeymoon can now tell their guests to visit WeddingChannel.com to assist them in purchasing the perfect gift—even a portion of the couple's trip of a lifetime.

> *"More and more couples are choosing to register for their honeymoon."*
>
> ADAM BERGER
> CEO

Top photo: Jamaica Tourist Board

Couples, too, benefit from Sandals' promotions and special events. Bridal promotions and events also help to spread the word about Sandals. Each year, Sandals partners with *Brides* magazine, offering prospective brides and grooms a preview of what it's like to honeymoon at one of the resorts. "About one thousand couples each year participate in these one-day getaways we call Test Drive Your Honeymoon," adds Rivera. "It gives couples a fun, hands-on opportunity to learn about destination weddings and honeymoons at one of the most popular resorts for both occasions."

And, there's nothing like a celebrity endorsement to help build a brand. Whether the superstars or sports legends are vacationing on their own or in town for one of Sandals' swanky celebrity happenings, the public loves knowing which famous faces have enjoyed a Sandals and Beaches stay. "Our celebrity events have been very successful, with the most recent one appearing on *Extra, E!*, and *Access Hollywood*, NBC's celebrity lifestyle television program," continues Rivera. "We've found that celebrities drive business and we are dedicated to continuing to produce major celebrity events."

GETTING IN THE GROOVE
Couples from around the country are on hand to "test drive" their honeymoon at Sandals.

"We wanted to create a **dynamic partnership** program whereby travel agents would be branded as '**certified**.'"

WELL-ASSEMBLED
Travel agents from across the country gather at Sandals Ultra Conventions to learn more about the #1 ultra all-inclusive resort group.

MADE IN THE TRADE

From 1981 through today, travel agents have been essential to selling Sandals vacations. Butch Stewart quickly realized that travel agents were the most qualified people to sell his resorts and, from the beginning, he built the brand with their help. Sandals ran an incredible amount of advertising in the "trade books" to make travel agents aware of the resort and keep them informed of the resort group's happenings. As the company matured, Sandals took the same approach with consumers. Nowadays, branding drives consumers to the travel agent; plus the agent, who is fully informed and educated, is sending clients to Sandals.

By 1996, the Sandals brand grew so strong that travel agents wanted to receive training and be able to tell clients they specialized in selling Sandals. "Based on demand, we began toying with the idea of developing our own franchise or consortium," says Mandy Chomat, senior vice president of sales and marketing for Unique Vacations. "We wanted to create a dynamic partnership program whereby travel agents would be branded as 'certified' and that would be something of value that we could provide to them and to consumers."

After months of refining, the Certified Sandals Specialist program was launched. Longtime members of the Unique Vacations team, Kim Sardo, Gordy Silverman and Maura Cecere, among others, helped develop the curriculum, which includes rigorous educational programs, marketing material customized to travel agents and special familiarization trips to the resorts so that agents can experience the resorts, and also a dedicated sales support staff.

"To be certified, travel agents have to undergo an intensive workshop training," explains Silverman. "We teach them everything they need to know about Sandals, from room categories to the number of restaurants at each property. Just as important, we also indoctrinate them into our corporate culture. Ultimately, it's all about ensuring that everyone, from staff to agent, goes the extra mile for guests."

To promote the program, Sandals created Ultra Conventions, party-like gatherings designed to inform and inspire agents into joining the ranks of Certified Sandals Specialists. "Travel agents remain our most vital business partner," says Chomat, "and we have a commitment to continue giving them the tools they need."

"Our job is to position and build the brand, articulate its unique differences, maintain its leadership, and make each product distinctive and desirable."

EFFECTIVE ADVERTISING AT ITS BEST

Sandals' award-winning advertising agency for more than a decade, Hunter-Hamersmith & Associates is the driving force behind Sandals vibrant look and brand leadership. Under the direction of Tracey Hunter and Cheryl Hamersmith, this savvy and creative shop produces the Sandals and Beaches collateral material, point-of-purchase displays, print advertising, outdoor billboards and television campaigns seen worldwide.

With strong marketing objectives and a flair for what consumers respond to, the agency developed Sandals' bold color scheme and distinctive design back in 1991. "No one was doing this at that time," recalls Tracey Hunter, "but we knew the advertising and collateral had to reflect the lively spirit and romantic charm of the Caribbean. We took a chance and Mr. Stewart loved the concept. It certainly received positive notice by consumers and has been effective ever since. Today, it's an often-copied style."

Sandals' distinctive style has evolved over the years, based on much hard work and dedication in continuing to build and re-invent the brand.

"We live the brand day in and day out, and we are there every step of the way, overseeing every detail," adds Hunter. "It has to do with our unwavering commitment and strong vision of brand definition. We love the challenge of continuing to create new ways to be the industry leader. We are also very mindful of what consumers are looking for and what they will respond to. A tremendous amount of what we do is instinctive but is also based on our long-term understanding of the brand."

BIG AND BOLD
Butch Stewart surrounded by colorful collateral created by advertising agency, Hunter Hamersmith & Associates

Adds partner Cheryl Hamersmith: "We've taken our cues from Butch Stewart. He is someone who listens to everyone because he considers everyone a potential consumer, from the man in the pinstripe suit to the fellow sweeping floors. We listen to him and we are able to get the essence of what he wants to convey. Our job is to position and build the brand, articulate its unique differences, maintain its leadership, and make each product distinctive and desirable. What we like most about creating the advertising is that while we're continually innovating, we find that a lot of other travel companies are following our lead. It's a terrific compliment."

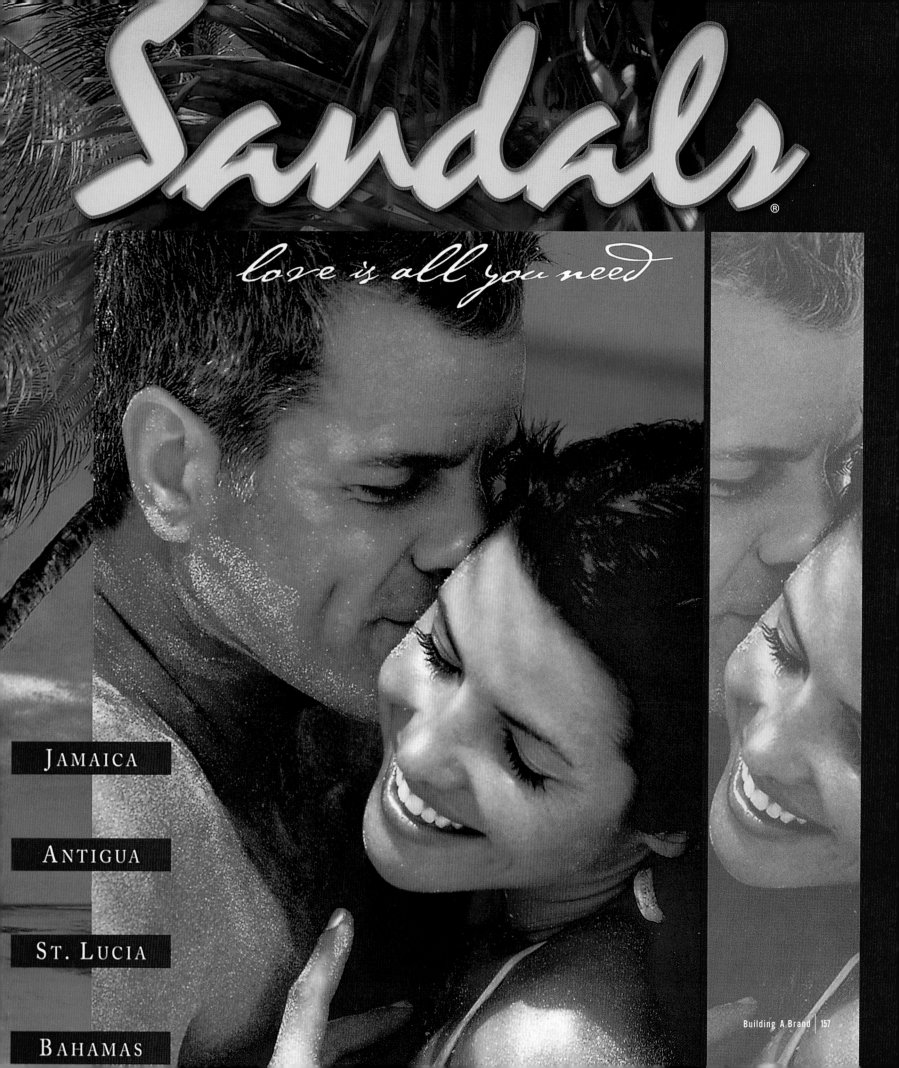

Sandals®

love is all you need

JAMAICA

ANTIGUA

ST. LUCIA

BAHAMAS

Getting There

Millions of people the world over make travel their quest in life. Luckily, *Travel + Leisure*, one of the world's leading travel magazine, speaks directly to them. "Our readers view us as the authority and the source that gets there first," says Nancy Novogrod, *Travel + Leisure*'s editor-in-chief. "Our authentic stories motivate our readers, making us the catalyst for setting trends."

The publication seeks to inform and inspire readers by searching out the newest and best in travel. And one alluring destination readers love to discover is the Caribbean, with all its beauty, romance and adventure.

"We cover the Caribbean extensively and are committed to uncovering all of the region's newest discoveries," says Ellen Asmodeo, vice president and publisher of *Travel + Leisure*. "We are also dedicated to the future of Caribbean travel and proudly support programs that contribute to its growth. Programs and partnerships, such as our involvement in the Caribbean Tourism Organization and its Youth Congress, continue to be examples of the strong and committed partnerships between *Travel + Leisure* and the Caribbean region."

One thing's certain, whether it's the Caribbean, Europe or any other part of the world, *Travel + Leisure* helps readers navigate the globe.

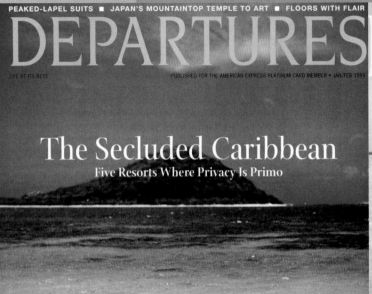

Departures

Departures

PEAKED-LAPEL SUITS ■ JAPAN'S MOUNTAINTOP TEMPLE TO ART ■ FLOORS WITH FLAIR

DEPARTURES DEPARTURES

LIFE AT ITS BEST PUBLISHED FOR THE AMERICAN EXPRESS PLATINUM CARD MEMBER • JAN/FEB 1999

OCTOBER 2003 $10.00

The Secluded Caribbean
Five Resorts Where Privacy Is Primo

Islands
Where To Go Next

Anguilla · Antigua · Bahamas · Barbados · Bequia · Bermuda · Bora-Bora
Capri · Corfu · Corsica · Curaçao · Dominican Republic · Fiji · Frégate
Galápagos · Gozo · Grenada · Guana · Hawaii · Hvar · Ibiza · Ischia
Jerba · Koh Lanta · Komodo · Langkawi · Lizard · Madeira · Maldives
Mallorca · Malta · Marquesas · Martinique · Mauritius · Mustique · Necker
Nevis · Panarea · Pangkor Laut · Phuket · Porquerolles · St. Barths
Seychelles · Tahaa · Tuamotus · Turtle · Virgin Gorda

When Platinum Card® and Centurion® Card members of American Express wish to seek insider recommendations and in-depth stories on the finest in travel, fashion, style, culture, recreation, and dining, they turn to *Departures* as their source. In its pages, affluent connoisseurs with sophisticated tastes read about all the very best that life has to offer.

Through the years, *Departures* has supported tourism growth to the Caribbean. The magazines' editorial team has covered the destination with a mix of lively and interesting articles. And readers have responded. In fact, *Departures* readers have returned to the Caribbean in even greater numbers these past two years, with a 23 percent increase in travel to the region.

> *"We applaud Butch Stewart and Sandals for twenty-plus years of sustainable tourism."*
>
> KATHI DOOLAN
> PUBLISHER

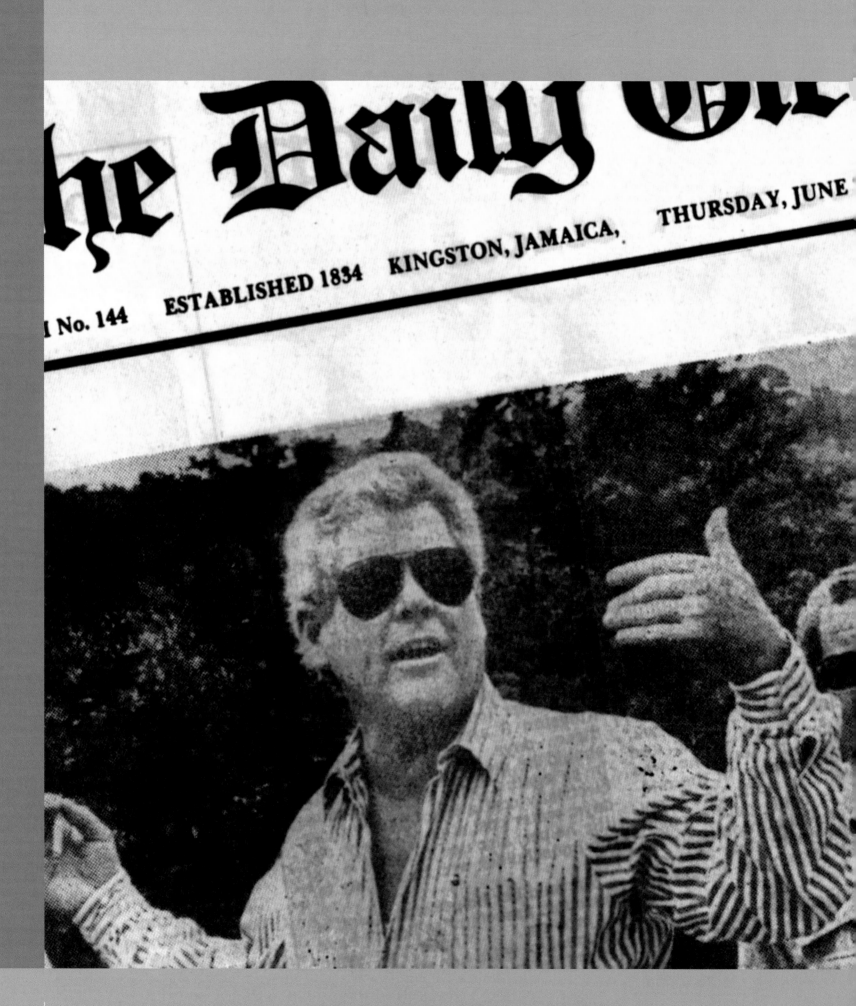

CHAPTER

6 Taking Initiative

MR. STEWART STARTED WITH ONE RUN-DOWN HOTEL AND WITHIN A FEW YEARS BUILT A HOTEL GROUP THAT IS UNDOUBTEDLY REGARDED ON A WORLD-WIDE BASIS AS THE STRONGEST AND MOST RECOGNIZED CARIBBEAN BRAND.

Dr. George Phillip
Vice President/Director
Sandals Resorts International

On Jamaica, bamboo rafting down the magnificent Rio Grande in Port Antonio first began in the 1870s. In those days, rafts provided a means of transportation, hauling bananas from plantations to Boundbrook Wharf where cargo ships awaited.

Seventy-five years later, in 1946, legendary movie star Errol Flynn happened upon the island when his yacht *Zacca* washed ashore during a storm. Instantly enamored, he made Port Antonio his second home. When he saw the river rafts, he considered modifying them into pleasure crafts. Soon enough, Flynn was floating leisurely down the river on lazy afternoons or inviting vacationing celebrities along for a day of partying and river racing.

Flynn's hedonistic notion spurred local tourism and fashioned entrepreneurs who developed businesses based on river rafting tours and other island activities. The seeds of private enterprise had been planted and, in the coming decades, they would extend throughout the region.

By the early 1990s throughout much of Latin America and the Caribbean, there was a spreading sentiment of individuality and self-reliance—a mind-set that people must determine their own economic future rather than rely on government. A new wave of self-help and private-sector undertakings was taking place. On Jamaica, a number of privatization and deregulation initiatives were under way, most important of which were the liberalization of currency and the abolishment of exchange control.

At last there was market freedom and free movement of currency into and out of the island, which was a new concept for Jamaicans. Many started to hoard dollars and stopped spending them in the market, preferring to speculate instead. Prices for goods skyrocketed, and the

Butch Stewart decided that "enough is enough."

Jamaican dollar was devaluing every day. Despite relative political and economic stability, the dollar crept from JA$10 equals US$1 to JA$30 equals US$1 in the space of eighteen months. Having deprived itself of the power to set the exchange rate by fiat, the government was in a quandary about what to do in a free market clearly gone wrong.

"The Jamaican dollar was collapsing and people were being savaged by high prices," recalls Patrick Lynch, a former international banker and now director of finance and planning for Sandals Resorts International. "There was also a general disrespect for the Jamaican dollar in what became a frenzy of speculation. It was a debilitating situation seemingly without solution."

STRONG SOLUTIONS
Opposite: Spurred on by Butch Stewart's Dollar Initiative, local banks run advertising to rally the nation with the hope of stabilizing the Jamaican dollar.

JOIN THE NATIONAL CAMPAIGN

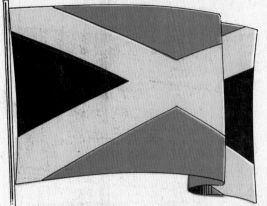

TO SAVE OUR DOLLAR

Sell your Foreign currency each Wednesday at any branch of National Commercial Bank islandwide and so contribute to the national

SAVE THE DOLLAR FUND

Join the people's initiative NOW and help stabilise our dollar!

Today, the rate of exchange is J$23.50 to 1US$.

Each week NCB, will announce the rate of purchase.

Help Stabilise our Jamaican dollar and Watch Jamaica Grow!!

NCB NATIONAL COMMERCIAL BANK JAMAICA LIMITED

TODAY

Helping to build a strong nation

"TRUE LEADERSHIP IS A RARE COMMODITY, PARTICULARLY IN LEADERS WHOSE POSITIVE INFLUENCE REACHES ALL CORNERS OF THE GLOBE. BUTCH STEWART IS ONE OF THOSE EXTRAORDINARY PEOPLE WHO HELPS BRING THE EXCELLENCE THAT EXISTS IN OUR REGION TO THE ATTENTION OF THE REST OF THE WORLD. HE AND THE REST OF THE SANDALS TEAM CONTINUE TO SET THE EXAMPLE FOR ENTREPRENEURS, COMMUNITY LEADERS, TRAVEL INDUSTRY MEMBERS, AND FOR OUR YOUTH. I AM GLAD THAT THEY WILL LEARN OF THE ACHIEVEMENTS OF THIS MAN AND HIS TALENTED ORGANIZATION, AND TRY TO FOLLOW THEIR EXAMPLE AND EMULATE THEIR ACCOMPLISHMENTS. I AM SURE THAT MORE OF THE CHALLENGES BUTCH STEWART THRIVES ON AWAIT HIM, AND I AM EQUALLY SURE THAT IN HIS OWN INIMITABLE STYLE, HE WILL SIMPLY RESPOND WITH FURTHER SUCCESS."

Peter J. July
Group Chairman
RBTT Financial Holdings Limited

RADICAL RESOLUTION

Sometimes, out of confusion the best ideas are formed. Early April, Butch Stewart decided that "enough is enough" and he formulated a response to the chaotic situation. That response, and the series of actions that followed, came to be known as the Jamaican Dollar Initiative, or the "Butch Initiative," and it would resuscitate the nation's confidence in itself.

Single-handedly, Gordon "Butch" Stewart came to the rescue of the Jamaican dollar. He stunned the nation on April 14, 1992, by publicly announcing at a press conference that, starting April 21, he would deposit US$1 million every week into Jamaica's commercial banks at a rate of JA$25 to US$1, rather than the then current rate of JA$30 to US$1, to help stop the slide of the Jamaican dollar.

"The move was dramatic and designed to shock the system in an effort to emphasize that enough is enough," explains Stewart. "I wanted to show that people can make a difference and that, to a great extent, the future depends on ourselves."

Brilliant and radical, the announcement hit the airwaves by storm. A number of journalists, especially Jamaica's popular talk-show hosts, took up the controversial subject and whipped up an enormous amount of public interest, education and discussion. Sensational debates took place on the radio, in the newspaper, on street corners, in offices, and in homes across the country. Everywhere, everybody was talking about one thing: the Dollar Initiative.

THE DOCTOR IS IN
Below left: Popular Jamaican radio host Leahcim Semaj was a strong advocate for the Dollar Initiative. Semaj, far right, interviews Stewart on air. The pair went on to become good friends. Above: Jamaicans line up at the bank to deposit foreign exchange.

WHAT DISTINGUISHES MR. STEWART IS THAT HE IS DEEPLY
ROOTED IN THE COUNTRY AND GENUINELY LOVES JAMAICA.
MOST PEOPLE JUST LIKE THE PLACE, BUT HE LOVES IT, WITH
ALL ITS DIVERSITY, INFINITE OPPORTUNITY, PROBLEMS,
AND CHALLENGES.

Patrick Lynch
Director of Finance & Planning
Sandals Resorts International

Public argument kept the initiative in the press and motivated the broad cross-section of the people, which is exactly the result Stewart was after. The initiative was hailed as ingenious by some and voodoo economics by others. One popular radio host, Dr. Leahcim Semaj, known as the "Night Doctor," viewed radio as a medium for change and challenged listeners to take up the initiative by depositing their foreign exchange into the banks: "One hundred thousand of us, at ten US dollars each, could match Butch Stewart's deposit weekly."

Now empowered and realizing they could make a difference, thousands of Jamaicans queued up with their dollars at banks across the nation to follow Stewart's lead.

"Within two days you had huge lines of people standing outside the banks to deposit their money at the Butch Stewart rate," recalls Lynch. "There were people from every walk of life—farmers and housekeepers, craft vendors and businessmen—ready to exchange five dollars or ten, or five hundred dollars. And several large companies announced similar measures. Collectively, their support created an avalanche, which forced the banks and the government to take notice."

Stewart started a revolution by defying traditional economics. He became a catalyst for making the greater Jamaican community realize that one person can make a difference. "You must understand that it was to his own great disadvantage to do this at the time because he was earning foreign exchange," notes Betty Jo Desnoes, Stewart's longtime executive assistant. "I think he felt that most of the people in the country would have benefited from a dollar that was set at twenty-five to one, and he did what had to be done: set the example by putting in his own money to stabilize the exchange rate." Indeed, the slide of the Jamaican dollar was halted and a stable exchange rate resulted for a very long time.

Organizing the orderly administration of the initiative through the banking system was left to Patrick Lynch. Many economic commentators as well as international agencies wanted to know the secret of how it worked. "They approached us looking for a formula," recalls Lynch. "But you can't repeat that process because there's no formula. The Dollar Initiative really was a very indigenous thing that arose out of our circumstances at the time. It was all based on national self-help in accordance with the prevailing thinking of the time, backed by the credibility of Butch Stewart and the deep respect in which he is held here."

"Yet again he set the standards, and through example displayed true national and community involvement," says Stewart's former wife, P. J. "He's not someone to isolate himself from the community in which he works, and he takes a stand in what he fully believes will support the greater good of the country."

"He takes a stand in what he fully believes will support the greater good of the country."

NATIONAL HONOR
Gordon "Butch" Stewart is awarded with the Commander of the Order of Distinction (CD) in August, 1988 at top, and the Order of Jamaica (OJ) in August, 1995 at right. These are two of Jamaica's highest national honors.

"We're proud to say that we have enjoyed a strong partnership with Sandals Resorts for more than twenty years."

STEVE GORGA
PRESIDENT

Lasting

Travel Impressions is proud to be celebrating its 30th anniversary as one of the largest tour operators in the United States.

Impressions

In 1967, Travel Impressions took root as a small retail travel agency called ATS, on Long Island, New York. A few years later, this small agency grew into a group incentive and convention company that offered trips from the Northeast United States to select destinations such as Cancun, Barbados and St. Maarten.

By 1974, Travel Impressions developed into an incorporated tour wholesaler, providing the traveling consumer with packaged vacation deals to the Caribbean and Mexico. Within ten years the tour business flourished: Travel Impressions went from selling three gateways to fifteen, and from representing five resorts to 150. Key to the growth and continued success of the company is its special relationship with, and value for, retail travel agents. "Our foundation and success is in our partnerships," says Travel Impressions Vice President of Sales Charles Gallina. "Our vast distribution channels, which include large retail travel agent chains as well as independent agencies, and their commitment to supporting a quality product is what drives consumers to our preferred partners."

Steve Gorga, President, Travel Impressions

As Butch Stewart was developing his all-inclusive resort on Jamaica in 1981, he quickly recognized that Travel Impressions was on the fast track to success and was becoming a national player in the travel wholesale business. Stewart approached the top brass at Travel Impressions and courted them to Jamaica to have a look at his fledgling all-inclusive resort, Sandals Montego Bay. The Travel Impressions team liked what they saw and so did Stewart. The relationship was solidified and it has been a successful alliance that has lasted twenty-three years.

As the Sandals phenomenon took off, so did Travel Impressions. Today, Travel Impressions is one of the nation's largest tour operators and travel wholesalers and a wholly-owned subsidiary of American Express Travel Related Service Company, Inc.

Elizabeth Beutel, a fifteen-year veteran of the company and Travel Impressions' director for marketing operations, comments: "I have had the privilege of watching the evolution of our company from a small family-owned travel business to becoming one of the largest travel wholesalers in the nation.

Travel Impressions delivers a diverse mix of travel packages that are dependable and flexible and offer value for money.

Through it all we have remained focused on delighting our customers and partners."

Still headquartered on Long Island, the company retains reservation call centers in New York, in Pennsylvania and in California.

Since its founding, Travel Impressions has serviced more than five million passengers and maintains a daily hotel inventory of approximately ten thousand hotel rooms at over twelve hundred hotels and resorts worldwide, including in the Caribbean, Mexico, Costa Rica, Florida, Las Vegas, New York, Hawaii, Panama, and Europe.

In addition, the company provides air-inclusive leisure packages from cities nationwide to its destinations, using scheduled air carriers such as American Airlines, Continental Airlines, Delta Air Lines, US Airways, and Air Jamaica.

As Travel Impressions celebrates its thirty-year anniversary in 2004, it has much to be proud of. Long regarded as a company that values the travel agent community, the Travel Impressions team continue to develop new products and services that allow

retail partners to be successful as the industry changes.

"Understanding our customers' expectations and responding quickly to their needs are paramount to the performance of Travel Impressions," says Roger Lagrone, Travel Impressions vice president, reservations. For example, Travel Impressions recently launched TI Connect, a private-label consumer booking engine, geared exclusively for travel agency Web sites. The program allows "non-tech" travel agencies to position themselves on the Internet with their own personalized booking system that delivers an easy-to-use, high-speed live inventory available 24/7.

Throughout its thirty-year history and an ever-changing marketplace, one constant has remained: Travel Impressions delivers a diverse mix of travel packages that are dependable and flexible and offer value for money. They are available only through travel agents.

A PROUD MOMENT: Entrepreneur and hotelier, Gordon "Butch" Stewart (r) accepts with pride, the 1992 Dr. Martin Luther King, Jnr. Award from Madge Barnett (L), secretary of the Jamaica America Society, while president, Henry Malliet, looks on. The award was presented to Stewart in recognition of his contribution in the fields of philanthropy, business and his commitment to the ideals of Dr. King, at the Martin Luther King, Jnr. Humanitarian Award ceremony, at the Wyndham Hotel in Kingston on Wednesday. — Cellmar photo

Jamaica Record, Jan 17 '92. PG.1

HIGH PRAISE
Butch Stewart and his executive assistant, Betty Jo Desnoes, are all smiles after he accepts the Dr. Martin Luther King Jr. Humanitarian Award.

A KING OF A MAN

Stewart served his country well as a catalyst for the Dollar Initiative. Though this act would establish him as a folk hero, there were hundreds of other endeavors that he undertook which also gave back to his community.

It is well known that the Reverend Dr. Martin Luther King Jr. inspired the world to serve humanitarian causes and ideals. In Jamaica, an annual award given in his name is bestowed on a distinguished Jamaican whose life and deeds best reflect the values of the distinguished civil rights leader.

When Gordon "Butch" Stewart received the prestigious Dr. Martin Luther King Jr. Humanitarian Award from the Jamaica-America Society on January 15, 1992, Dr. King's birthday, people were made even more aware of Stewart's contribution.

During the ceremony, held at the Wyndham Kingston Hotel, Stewart was cited for his role in creating more than 2,700 jobs in Jamaica and for one of his best-kept secrets—his philanthropic endeavors, a subject he is reluctant to talk about.

Jamaica's governor-general at the time, Sir Howard Cooke, praised Stewart at the ceremony: "Butch is a person of great merit, a philanthropist, bringing relief and comfort to people in need."

Indeed, Stewart's generosity has helped thousands. He has donated millions of dollars in cash, services and materials to religious, educational, civic and charitable organizations such as the Salvation Army, March of Dimes, Red Cross, Boy Scouts, Y.M.C.A., and numerous hospitals, clinics and children's homes. Stewart is not only responsible for building and maintaining schools and colleges throughout Jamaica, but he also sends Santa on visits each year at Christmas with toys and goodies for nearly one thousand underprivileged Jamaican children.

William Mahoney, then president of the American Chamber of Commerce, told the audience at the ceremony, "Like Martin Luther King, Butch is a man among men, inspiring greatness in people, working hard and persevering on the side of ideals and justice and the principles in which he believes."

DR. MARTIN LUTHER KING JR. AWARDS BANQUET

Jamaica-America Society SOUVENIR '92

Money Matters

While Sandals expanded its resort properties on St. Lucia, the island's financial sector did some pacesetting too. In July 2001, the merger of the National Commercial Bank of St. Lucia (NCB) and the Saint Lucia Development Bank (SLDB) gave birth to the island's largest conglomerate: the East Caribbean Financial Holding Company Limited, with The Bank of Saint Lucia Limited as the group's main subsidiary. The new arrangement made it possible for The Bank of Saint Lucia to expand into new areas of finance, including investments and insurance.

With the catchphrase "All the bank you need," Bank of Saint Lucia has stepped up as the standard-bearer for national development. Since its creation, the bank has endeavored to be a catalyst for indigenous banks in the Organization of Eastern Caribbean States and has ventured to expand its horizons beyond.

Among its many services, Bank of Saint Lucia provides traditional deposit and lending services, corporate banking and foreign business. It is also one of the few regional banks providing development banking services, attracting funding regionally and internationally to assist in the development of the productive and social sectors of St. Lucia.

As good corporate citizens, the bank has a strong commitment to social, economic and cultural development on St. Lucia, making significant monetary contributions toward educational, environmental, sporting and cultural development, and community outreach programs within the region.

With more than 270 staff, The Bank of Saint Lucia blends two of the largest institutions on St. Lucia. The partnership was developed to help expand public- and private-sector partnerships through shareholdings within and across national boundaries.

Bank of Saint Lucia blends two of the largest institutions on St. Lucia.

As Sandals Resorts approached its tenth anniversary, there was much to celebrate. Trailblazing was a Sandals specialty and now it led the pack in the all-inclusive market. Once again, a new destination was sought. The emerald island of St. Lucia beckoned.

The island's jade-green mountains are sprinkled with color from violet orchids and yellow-green banana-plant leaves. Lush rain forests blanket the landscape and cover the striking landmark peaks of the twin Pitons, rising 2,600 feet. Complementing the greenery are magnificent beaches, mineral-rich baths and quiet fishing villages.

In essence, it was an ideal destination to open the eighth Sandals resort.

St. Lucia

MAKING THE CUT
From left: Former St. Lucia Prime Minister Sir John Compton and his wife join Butch Stewart and his wife then, P.J., at the ribbon-cutting ceremony for Sandals St. Lucia. Below: A rendering of Sandals St. Lucia, soon to be a dramatic new resort.

ST. LUCIA SHINES

St. Lucia's charismatic director of tourism at the time, Allen Chastanet, courted the Sandals group. "I met Mr. Stewart in 1990 at a Caribbean Hotel Association meeting and mentioned to him that St. Lucia would love to have Sandals come to its shores," recalls Chastanet. "Mr. Stewart responded that if there was ever an opportunity, to get in touch with him. When Cunard's La Toc property went for sale in 1992, we made contact. Mr. Stewart and his team were impressed with the charming property. They promised to raise the exposure of the island and to elevate the hotel to another level. And they certainly lived up to that."

"Our feeling was that if you're going to be a Caribbean destination, you need to round off," recalls Sandals' Patrick Lynch, "and St. Lucia gave us a lot of opportunities. We wanted to be on St. Lucia and negotiated with Cunard to acquire the property."

When the ink was dry, Sandals sent in its crack executive and projects team—newly named General Manager Louis Grant; architect Evan Williams; project managers Larry McDonald, Andre McDonald and Eleanor Miller; interior designer Sue Cronin; and many others—to get started on what would be a $20 million renovation.

"This setting was magnificent and, above all, Mr. Stewart wanted to build a totally glamorous resort," recalls project director Andre McDonald. "We used a lot of marble and very fine furnishings. All of the public areas were redone and the pool was just outrageous."

"ONE OF THE WONDERFUL THINGS ABOUT SANDALS IS THAT IT HAS CREATED A REAL CARIBBEAN HOTEL CULTURE. THE COMPANY BELIEVES IN HIRING LOCALS, TRAINING THEM, AND BRINGING THEM UP THROUGH THE MANAGEMENT LEVEL. TAKE ST. LUCIA, FOR EXAMPLE. BUTCH STEWART IS COMMITTED TO ENSURING THAT ST. LUCIANS FIRST AND FOREMOST RISE TO THE CHALLENGE AND ASSUME MANAGEMENT AND LEADER-SHIP ROLES WITHIN THE ORGANIZATION. THAT IS DONE AT ALL HIS PROPERTIES AT EVERY DESTINATION AND I BELIEVE IT ADDS A SPECIAL DIMENSION TO THE HOTEL GROUP."

Berthia Parle
President
Caribbean Hotel Association

"Every time we start to work on a property, it's going to pop."

"Butch wanted a property that was absolutely unique, unlike any other. He wanted it to be grand and incredibly glamorous," remembers architect Evan Williams. "At the time, this was to be the showcase property, so we figured, why not build the biggest pool we can imagine to complement the beautiful beach and scenery. Then, guests can immerse themselves in the Caribbean, look at the sea and enjoy. When we took over the property, it didn't have a proper lobby or entrance, and the dining room was quite small. Our challenge was how to marry a new lobby with an entertainment area, dining room, pool, beach and the sea and give it all a sense of drama."

SHOWSTOPPER
The striking scale and proportion of the main dining room at Sandals Regency St. Lucia Golf Resort & Spa make it an outstanding focal point of the property.

"Every time we start to work on a property, it's going to pop," states Betty Jo Desnoes. "If it doesn't come in the beginning, it comes halfway through. We're always looking for something to give that property a unique personality. And Mr. Stewart starts with the visual, which is his advertising bent. If you try to rationalize some of the things he wants to build or to create, you can't. Perhaps they're not practical, but that's the vision. He knows what he wants, and that's what he's going to use to market that property."

SLICE AND DICE
Guests enjoy Japanese food and the entertaining chef at Kimonos, in a splendid setting overlooking the sea at Sandals Regency St. Lucia Golf Resort & Spa.

Where Stewart chose to build his new Japanese restaurant did not seem that sensible at first. "There's a part of the hillside on property that was not developed when we got there. This is where the chairman decided he wanted us to build Kimonos, up high on the side of this cliff," recalls Andre McDonald. "We all thought he was mad because there's just no way the structure was there to support it. It just didn't make sense. Everyone advised him against it, but he did it anyway. Mr. Stewart is not interested in hearing why not. He is only interested in hearing how. That restaurant appears to be floating in space and offers guests the most amazing views of the sea. In hindsight, it *was* the perfect setting."

Kimonos is just one of many appealing amenities. There is also a nine-hole golf course, sixty suites and three other gourmet restaurants. The real stunner, however, is the quarter-acre main swimming pool and dining area, which offers a visual feast and "pops" like nothing else before it.

"One of the things we were after was to ensure that the property was photogenic, so that when people saw a photograph of it they would say, 'Wow, what is this place about? We have to go.' The style is inspired by famed Italian Renaissance architect Palladio," says Evan Williams. "He had an incredible sense of classical scale and proportion, absolutely dwarfing the individual yet giving something they could relate to. Hence the dining room ceilings at Sandals Regency are thirty-eight feet high. We designed the structure so that from the dining room you could step right into the pool. It was all based on a fantasy of some exotic person going swimming, coming out of the pool and then straight into a dining room."

"Mr. Stewart always wants things over the top, nothing subtle," muses Eleanor Miller. "He likes very lush tropical landscaping and he wants luxury. He feels very strongly that the notion of getting better and better is a part of survival in the industry. And, he's moved the bar up many times at Sandals in terms of innovations and standards."

SINGING SANDALS' PRAISES
Below left: Jazz musician
Herbie Hancock, center, "plays"
at the Sandals Regency St. Lucia
Grand Opening while former
St. Lucia Prime Minister Sir John
Compton, left, and former St. Lucia
Director of Tourism Allen Chastanet
look on.

Proficient Patti

"Every year I raise the bar higher, and every year I surpass it." That's the winning attitude of Patti LaBella, an achiever who is one of Sandals' top-selling travel agents. Based in Stamford, Connecticut, this one-woman travel phenomenon has been selling Sandals exclusively since her start in the industry. "I wanted to be affiliated with a high-caliber product," explains LaBella.

Regarded as one of the most knowledgeable agents selling Sandals, LaBella at first "did not have a clue what Sandals was about" when she started in the business in 1996. That changed within days. "One day I received a call from a client wanting to spend his honeymoon at Sandals St. Lucia," says LaBella. "When I familiarized myself with the company and reviewed its marketing material, I decided to specialize and sell only Sandals."

LaBella immersed herself in the business, learning everything she could about Sandals and Beaches. She studied room categories and property layouts and traveled to all the resorts. Within months, she became a Certified Sandals Specialist. "Knowledge is power," declares LaBella, a consultant who is intensely passionate about her business.

"I am determined to continue being the best agent and to provide my clients with an excellent vacation experience."

PATTI LABELLA
OWNER

States Mandy Chomat, senior vice president of sales and marketing for Unique Vacations, "Patti is a top agent who shares our vision. She goes the extra mile for every one of her clients, ensuring they have a memorable honeymoon or vacation."

Celebrated for her achievements at the first annual Sandals Travel Agent Recognition Awards and honored with a suite named after her at Sandals Regency St. Lucia, LaBella looks forward to growing along with Sandals. "I feel the best is yet to come and I want to continue being part of it," says LaBella. "Most importantly, I want my clients to know that when they book with me, they've selected the best."

Photo: Sandals Resorts International

"Butch believed
there was truly a need for
another paper, one with a
community flavor."

MAKING NEWS

Butch Stewart has made headlines throughout his business career. But in July 1992, the concept of making news took a different turn. At the time, Dr. George Phillip, executive director for Sandals Resorts International, listened intently one evening as Stewart talked about why he thought he wanted to start a national newspaper.

Phillip recalls, "Butch felt that not enough was being done in terms of education and community development, and he wanted to create a vehicle through which he could highlight important initiatives and success stories coming out of Jamaica. Butch believed there was truly a need for another paper, one with a community flavor."

Though the well-established and distinguished *Jamaica Gleaner* had been the national newspaper since 1834, the time had arrived for Jamaica to get another point of view in print. Many competing radio and television stations were successful on the island, but there was only one definitive national newspaper.

Phillip continues: "After thoughtful consideration, Stewart joined forces with Delroy Lindsey, a banker, who had also wanted to form a paper, although none of them knew a thing about the newspaper business! Luckily they hired Ken Gordon, who was managing director at the *Trinidad Express*, to provide editorial and technical support."

On January 15, 1993, the Jamaica Observer Limited was officially launched as an organization with the notion of creating a national newspaper that would be apolitical, balanced in news presentation, strong on national issue opinions, and educational and developmental in terms of the community.

The Jamaica Observer proudly published its first weekly paper on March 5, 1993. Nineteen months later, on December 11, 1994, it went daily.

Even in print, Stewart led the way. "We were the first weekly paper to come out in color," boasts Phillip. "We had sixteen pages of full color the first day we published. Back then it was unique and considered an innovation."

"The paper continues to highlight individual initiatives," comments Phillip. "We developed the Business Leader of the Year award, which recognizes Jamaica's outstanding entrepreneurs. *The Jamaica Observer*'s community-service program features individuals and organizations that make a concerted effort to help the community. Another strong focus is on Jamaica's teens. We're committed to featuring articles that help give teenagers a leg up and keep them informed, whether it be profiles on successful teens or our Tuesday paper, which includes a teenage study guide to assist with schoolwork."

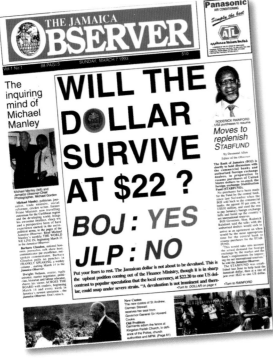

HOT OFF THE PRESS
The Jamaica Observer **hit the newsstands on March 5, 1993, at first as a weekly paper.**

7

The World's Best

TO BE RECOGNIZED BY TRAVEL AGENTS AROUND THE WORLD AS BEING THE TOP CARIBBEAN HOTEL GROUP AND WORLD'S LEADING INDEPENDENT RESORT IS TREMENDOUS. THIS IS A TRUE TESTAMENT NOT ONLY TO OUR RESORT GROUP BUT ALSO TO THE CARIBBEAN.

John D. Lynch
Executive Vice President Sales Worldwide
Unique Vacations

Winsome Grant wanted to go home. Having lived in Atlanta, Georgia, for several years, she was ready to return to Jamaica. She missed the Jamaican way of life, her family and friends, and the amicable tight-knit community she grew up in.

For the occasion of her homecoming in April 1995, Grant chose to travel on Air Jamaica. Through the years, she remained loyal to Jamaica's carrier.

The day she approached the ticket counter at Hartsfield Atlanta International Airport, Grant took note of the red carpet rolled out under her feet and the bright new uniform worn by Errol James, the ticket agent behind the counter. "Welcome to the new Air Jamaica," he greeted her. "Your flight is on time. Proceed to gate 5." When the aircraft pulled up to the jetway, Winsome glimpsed the new Airbus painted bold yellow, orange, blue, and magenta. She heard that the national airline had recently been privatized and that impressive innovations were taking place. Later that afternoon as the jet landed on time at Kingston's Norman Manley International Airport, she felt prouder to be Jamaican. Winsome Grant was happy to be home.

TIME TO FLY

What began as a small national carrier in April 1969—with flights between Kingston and Montego Bay and New York and Miami—developed over the years into a significant airline. By the early 1990s, however, the government of Jamaica, which had run Air Jamaica for more than twenty years, sought to divest; a majority stake of Air Jamaica was put up for sale.

It was June 23, 1994, when reports first began to appear in *The Jamaica Observer* and the *Jamaica Gleaner* that leading Caribbean hotelier Butch Stewart might be a potential private investor in Air Jamaica. The speculation was welcomed by those in the travel industry, who viewed Stewart as a proven leader with the marketing savvy and skills to direct the Jamaica flag carrier. "He has a track record of success and extremely close ties to the major tour operators and retail agents who sell the Caribbean," reported *Travel Weekly*, a travel industry trade publication.

Together with the Air Jamaica Acquisition Group, a group of private investors, Stewart paid $37.5 million for 70 percent of the carrier. Butch Stewart held a majority interest of 46 percent and was named chairman of Air Jamaica.

"Air Jamaica must be a viable organization in order to serve the tourist industry and the people of Jamaica," Stewart said at the time. "We are pleased to have an opportunity to support the revitalization of a national asset."

On November 15, 1994, the transfer of ownership was completed and the "new" Air Jamaica was born.

"I bought into Air Jamaica because it is part of the economy," elaborates Stewart. "Islands that do not have their own airline are in trouble. They will always be at the mercy of foreign carriers. From a national perspective it is critical to have an aggressive national carrier pioneering and doing the legwork. Although it was a huge challenge, we knew we had to make an enormous impact."

> ## "We are pleased to support the revitalization of a national asset."

READY FOR TAKEOFF
Above: Butch Stewart, left, poses with the new Air Jamaica team. Opposite: Airline moguls Sir Richard Branson of Virgin Atlantic and Butch Stewart of Air Jamaica.

Stewart went full throttle revamping the airline. Old planes were sold off and replaced by new, colorfully painted Airbus jets. Services and training were revitalized at the now "on-time, no-line" airline. Hot meals, champagne service and expanded routes were just some of the innovations taking place. An all-out marketing campaign with fresh brochures, billboards and in-flight videos appealed to Jamaicans' national pride. Surely, Air Jamaica had found its managerial leadership.

"We want Air Jamaica to be a true national carrier for one and all Jamaicans," says Stewart. "I regard our time, effort and investment in the airline to be one of national service."

MODERN ATTIRE
Butch Stewart unveils Air Jamaica's colorful new Airbus fleet poised for takeoff.

Harris Paints (St. Lucia) Ltd.

Colors of the Caribbean

The Caribbean distinguishes itself by its lush landscape and magnificent colors reflected by the sun and the water. Emerald may be the predominant color on the island of St. Lucia, a destination regarded for its verdant scenery, but an array of striking hues dot the landscape as well. Sunset yellow, warm-breeze blue, hibiscus-flower pink, and other tropical colors can be found both in interiors and exteriors at Sandals' properties on St. Lucia.

Harris Paints St. Lucia has been painting the interiors and exteriors at Sandals since the hotel group first came to the island in 1992. "We've been delighted to bring color to Sandals' resorts and enhance the St. Lucian landscape," says Keith Smith, managing director of Harris Paints St. Lucia, "and we feel the combination has contributed to the Caribbean experience that so many vacationers seek."

"We've been delighted to bring color to Sandals' resorts and enhance the St. Lucian landscape."

KEITH SMITH
MANAGING DIRECTOR

Photo: Sandals Resorts International

"A COMMON THREAD RUNS THROUGH OUR GROUP OF COMPANIES—THE PROVISION OF SERVICE OVER AND ABOVE THE CUSTOMER'S EXPECTATION. EVERYTHING WE'RE INVOLVED IN IS DUE TO MR. STEWART'S VISION, HIS CLEARLY OUTLINED IMAGE OF HOW HIS COMPANIES SHOULD BE RUN. IT'S BEEN INGRAINED IN ME AND THAT'S WHAT I TRY TO EMULATE IN TERMS OF RUNNING THE COMPANIES."

Chris Zacca
Deputy Chairman
ATL Group of Companies

REACHING HIGHER ALTITUDES

Stewart profoundly understood that the need for a successful national airline is critical to the Caribbean's tourist-based economy—and especially to a hotelier with an ever-growing portfolio of resorts.

By mid-1994, Sandals had expanded its hotel operations significantly, enhanced its guest services and solidified travel agent relations. Recent initiatives had included the opening of a second resort on St. Lucia, named Sandals Halcyon Beach Resort, which opened in May 1994. The resort proved to be an ideal complement to Sandals St. Lucia.

"We were starting to build our brand in the Eastern Caribbean," says Konrad Wagner, the first general manager of Sandals Halcyon, "and we wanted to ensure that we offered guests a range of vacation choices, which has always been important to us."

Indeed, with its low-key, laid-back atmosphere, Sandals Halcyon, a postcard-perfect resort by the sea, was well-matched beside the opulent and dramatic setting of Sandals Regency St. Lucia, a mere ten-minute drive up the road through the capital of Castries.

PEAK PERFORMANCE
St. Lucia's lush landscape, pictured opposite, proved to be a perfect backdrop for Sandals. In May 1994, the hotel group opened its second resort on the island, Sandals Halcyon Beach St. Lucia, pictured above.

"St. Lucia was up and coming by this time," St. Lucia's former director of tourism, Allen Chastanet, points out. "And Sandals deserves a lot of the credit for helping to raise the profile of the destination. We were just blown away by the level of support and marketing they came in with. The island of St. Lucia received credibility in the U.S. market and moved further into the European market backed by this tremendous brand with its phenomenal reputation in the travel arena."

As leaders in the all-inclusive market, the Sandals team behind the scenes was constantly at work pioneering new concepts and amenities for their guests. Now, the brand that started in 1981 with a resort designed for "two people in love" was about to become even more romantic.

St. Lucia Tourist Board

Simply Beautiful

The island of St. Lucia appeals to travelers seeking pleasure and enrichment—the wonder of the undiscovered, the adventure of the unfamiliar and the stimulation of the exotic. The island's natural beauty and one-of-a-kind sights distinguish St. Lucia from its Caribbean neighbors. The friendliness and vibrant cultural heritage of its people are also among the island's greatest assets.

Promoting and marketing this "simply beautiful" island to would-be travelers falls under the responsibility of the St. Lucia Tourist Board, a team of professionals who are at your service to assist with enquiries about the island and all its delights.

"St. Lucia offers a variety of attractions to the sophisticated traveler and a diverse lodging choice, including Sandals all-inclusives, which have added appeal to the destination," says Hilary Modeste, director of tourism.

Here Comes the Sun

There is perhaps no tour wholesaler in Canada whose history parallels that of the growing travel industry more closely than Signature Vacations. In 1972, when, as Adventure Tours, the organization started offering packages out of Toronto, cruise ships still regularly sailed the Atlantic and the first jumbo jet had rolled off the assembly line. The company quickly gained a name for itself by offering convenient and affordable packages to sun destinations specializing in the then-new concept of all-inclusive resorts.

Eventually, Adventure Tours purchased a number of well-established regional tour operators in Vancouver, Winnipeg and Montreal, giving the group a unique national presence. Then in 1994, First Choice Holidays PLC of Great Britain, one of the world's leading leisure travel companies, acquired the group, giving it enormous negotiating power in contracting hotel rooms and air seats. The following year, the Canadian group was re-branded as Signature Vacations.

Starting in 2000, the company set out on a path of vertical integration and has since acquired an array of travel agencies across Canada, marketing the best in leisure travel, including all-inclusive packages. "We've been selling all-inclusives for more than thirty years," says Signature Vacations Vice President of Sales and Marketing Mary Heron, "so it's no surprise that we're 'sold' on Sandals and Beaches. Excellent product, tremendous service and always exciting new developments."

Today, Signature Vacations is recognized and trusted for its high standards of service and quality. The travel group enjoys the support of consumers and travel agents across Canada in its expanding leisure travel activities.

By the mid-'90s, many couples were forsaking traditional weddings and whisking away to **exotic destinations** to tie the knot.

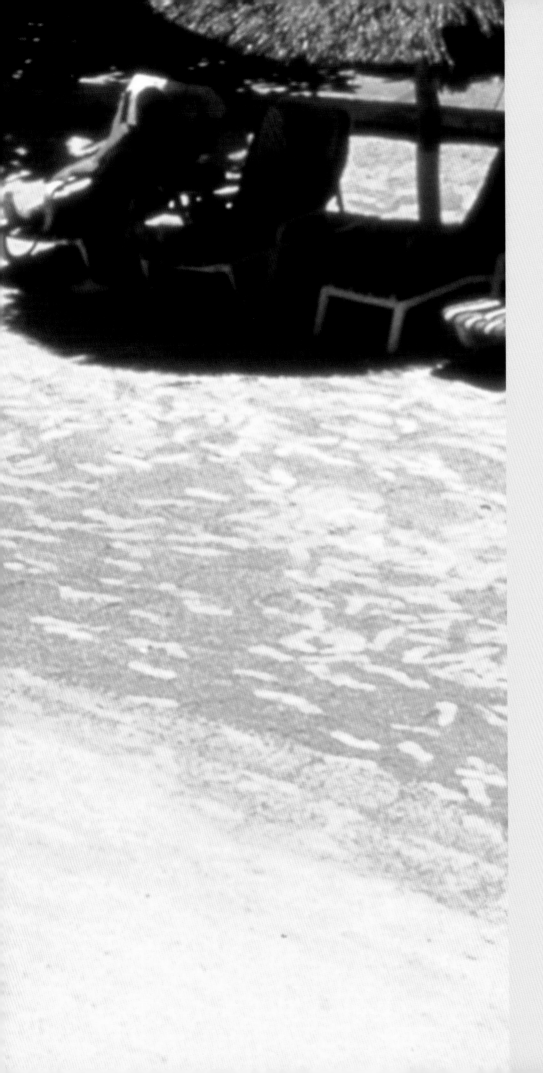

For many young couples and for those choosing to get married later in life, and for some marrying for the second time or simply renewing their vows, the notion of a romantic, hassle-free wedding away is quite alluring.

Following a trend the bridal industry termed "destination weddings," Sandals introduced WeddingMoons™, a variety of wedding package options that allow couples to marry and honeymoon at any Sandals resort. "We've been in the business of weddings for a long time," says John Lynch, executive vice president of sales worldwide for Unique Vacations and brainchild of the WeddingMoon™ concept. "WeddingMoons are a natural for us, given the trend we've seen over the last few years. The Sandals honeymoon begins the moment a couple says, 'I do.' We took that appeal and created a range of truly special and romantic wedding packages that will be remembered long after the ceremony has ended."

Saying "I do" to WeddingMoons™, they did—by the thousands. The concept has sparked a booming wedding business for Sandals, as couples from around the world travel to the Caribbean to get married under a gazebo by the beach or have a wedding extravaganza at one of Sandals' private villas. Yet again, the innovative resort group took a leading role in a growing trend.

*Romantic, yet real,
Bride's strong
journalistic approach
and visual sophistication
engage the reader's
interest and evoke a
powerful response.*

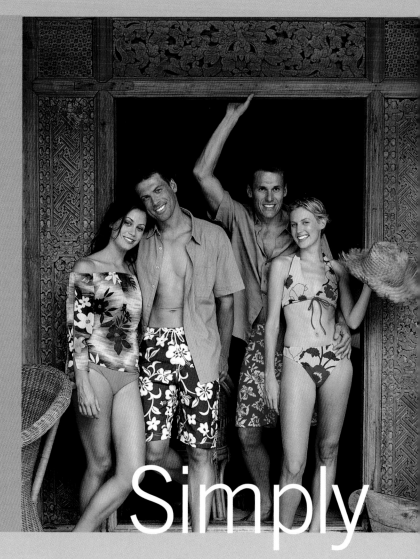

Simply

**The Condé Nast Bridal Group
has created a dominant
force in lifestage marketing.**

By uniting the strongest titles in bridal publishing under one powerful umbrella, the Condé Nast Bridal Group has created a dominant force in lifestage marketing. The combination of *Bride's, Modern Bride* and *Modern Bride Connection*, along with unparalleled event opportunities and complementary online sites, provides marketers access to nearly 97 percent of the bridal market. And, it provides clout to attract the undivided attention of the 8.2 million consumers who fuel the $120 billion bridal industry.

Engaging

The aura of *Bride's* magical editorial focus is at the center of the magazine's extraordinary relationship with its readers. *Bride's* opens up a world of fantasy to brides of all ages and circumstances. Romantic, yet real, *Bride's* strong journalistic approach and visual sophistication engage the reader's interest and evoke a powerful response. Within its pages, dreams can be realized and issues that impact the start of married life can be resolved. *Bride's*, the first wedding magazine of its kind, is the authority on all things bridal—a captivating voice that speaks with elegance and finesse to engaged couples.

Creative and provocative, *Modern Bride* is a smart, funny, slightly irreverent magazine that speaks to the bride in a fresh, new way. A breezy, vivacious editorial style is spiked with a sense of humor as well as an eye for practicality. Talking girlfriend-to-girlfriend, *Modern Bride* shares insights and ideas about the things readers want to know

in a witty, friendly way, and maybe even breaks a few traditional rules. By understanding the range of reader interests and the commitment each bride has to begin her new life with verve and enthusiasm, *Modern Bride* embraces and celebrates the exciting "engagement" lifestage in every issue.

Now in its seventh year, "World's Best Honeymoons," an exciting, informative and highly popular feature in *Modern Bride*, reveals the results of an independent survey of over three thousand ASTA travel agents who specialize in honeymoon travel. The survey ranks honeymoon destinations in categories such as "most romantic," "best spots for destination weddings," "best for beaches," "best for nightlife," "trendiest destinations," and much more.

Sandals is featured in "World's Best All-Inclusives" every year from 1997 through 2004 of this annual survey.

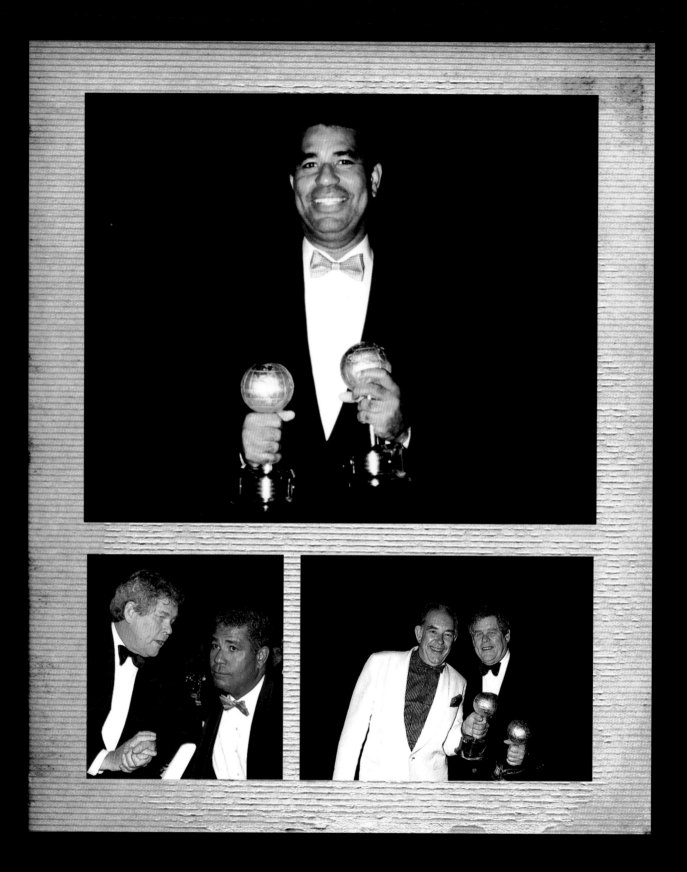

'THE' CHOICE FOR AGENTS

Sandals' position in the travel market was clear: It was the leading ultra all-inclusive resort group in the Caribbean. And as far as travel agents were concerned, well, Sandals was definitely number one in their books. Why? The high quality of the product, the unprecedented choice and the latest, greatest innovations.

"One of the advantages of working for Sandals and calling on travel agents is that we always have something new to tell them, whether it's the latest resort, room category or gourmet specialty restaurant," remarks Kim Sardo, a longtime member of the Unique Vacations team. "So while other travel companies may become complacent, we never will, and it's always a pleasure to have something new to say and to sell."

The ongoing love affair between Sandals and the travel community became even more pronounced one evening in November 1994. It was on the backlot at Universal Studios in California, where nearly 1,400 world travel industry movers and shakers gathered for the first annual World Travel Awards. Travel agents in over fifty countries had cast their vote and the results were in: Sandals Resorts won two prestigious awards—World's Leading Independent Resort and Top Caribbean Hotel Group.

TRAVEL KUDOS
Butch Stewart, Sandals senior staffers and industry friends celebrate as Sandals Resorts International takes top honors at the 1994 World Travel Awards ceremony in Los Angeles.

love

I know why Sandals is such a success. I'll tell you why. Just sit in the lobby at any resort and watch departing guests. I did that at Sandals Montego Bay once. Two honeymoon couples were preparing to depart. Some Sandals staffers came to say good-bye. There were hugs, solemn promises to return next year and real tears! It's a thing, I think, called love—between a young couple and a Sandals staffer who were best friends for a week. All were embracing and choking back tears. That's what travel is all about.

LARRY CAFIERO
EDITOR
SOUTHEAST TRAVEL PROFESSIONAL
IN MEMORIAM

As Sandals became an international resort group with representatives throughout Europe, the number of global guests flocking to its shores grew in leaps and bounds. With guests speaking a variety of languages, initially the staff on property had a dialogue dilemma. So to make international visitors feel at home, the team at Sandals Resorts International created an Ambassador Program, recruiting energetic European-based hotel-school graduates to work in various departments on property. "It has always been important for us to make guests feel welcome," says Merrick Fray, managing director for Sandals Resorts International. "The Ambassador Program is a natural extension of that philosophy. Our program has gone from strength to strength and it is fantastic that we now have staff at all our resorts that understand the nuances of language and culture." Thanks to the "ambassadors," staff speaking in Japanese, Italian, Spanish, French, German, Norwegian, Swedish, Danish, Portuguese, Dutch, and Russian can be heard at Sandals and Beaches resorts.

AMBASSADORS AWAIT

"Konnichi wa. Bonjour. Buenos días." No matter how guests may say it, Sandals Ambassadors, pictured at left with senior staffers, speak their language.

Sandals Ambassadors at Sandals Resorts International, Montego Bay

Protection & Security

Rest Assured

Guests at Sandals and Beaches resorts rest easy while on their vacation thanks to the trusted team at Protection & Security Limited. The Jamaican company has been providing security services for enterprises in the fields of hospitality, agriculture and education and in residential and commercial industries for more than thirty-five years.

"Our company offers manpower and electronic and courier security services throughout Jamaica," says Dennis Morgan, chief executive officer. "We are dedicated to providing top-notch security products and services of a world-class standard to meet the needs of our clients."

Based on Hope Road in Kingston, the company has a professional staff of more than one thousand officers. "Our staff receives extensive training not only in protective services but also in customer relations, which is very important for our business," adds Dennis Morgan. "Especially in the hospitality industry, our goal is to make sure that guests at the hotel feel totally safe and secure."

Sandals Antigua Caribbean Village & Spa

Photo: Sandals Resorts International

Beaches Turks & Caicos Resort & Spa

All-Inclusive at Its Best

Go Classy Tours, sellers of upscale Caribbean all-inclusive resort vacations, has been in business for more than fifteen years handling vacation reservations for families, couples and singles. When it sends clients to Sandals and Beaches resorts, the company says it knows they will be treated with an extra personal touch.

"Mr. Stewart trained his staff very well and they certainly know how to pamper their guests," says Andrea Hutchinson, president of Go Classy Tours. "I witnessed this firsthand on a trip to Beaches." Hutchinson and her young daughter had spent a memorable week at Beaches Turks and Caicos. Upon their departure from the resort, the housekeeping staff noticed that Hutchinson's daughter left her beloved stuffed bear behind in the room. They rushed teddy to the airport in a taxicab, but it was too late. The plane had already taken off. The driver returned the bear to the hotel general manager, who promptly shipped teddy home overnight.

"It's very reassuring for us to know that, like we were treated, our clients will be treated, with such care," says Hutchinson. "We've enjoyed a long and close working relationship with Butch Stewart and the Sandals team and are very proud of the team that operates the properties."

"First and foremost, Sandals caters to its guests."

ANDREA HUTCHINSON
PRESIDENT

Tara Hutchinson at age 3 clutches her beloved bear and at age 16.

Top photo: Sandals Resorts International

Booking your travel to the Caribbean aboard Air Jamaica is "no problem" with Air Jamaica Vacations.

Gateway to

Signature Lovebird hospitality to ensure that passengers receive the best possible airline experience.

the Caribbean

Air Jamaica has come a long way from its start as a small national carrier. Jamaica's flagship carrier has been flying the skies since 1969, but the airline really took off in 1994, when an acquisition group led by Gordon "Butch" Stewart privatized the airline.

From then on, the airline began to modernize its fleet and focus on service. The goal was to revitalize the spirit of air travel by increasing in-flight services and enhancing technology. A variety of improvements were introduced—vibrant aircraft and livery; expanded on-board amenities such as complimentary beer, wine and champagne on every flight; upgraded meal service supervised by the world's only "Flying Chef"; and red carpet check-in.

Air Jamaica's signature Lovebird hospitality strives to ensure that passengers receive the best possible airline experience, with personalized attention from the time of check-in through to deplaning. And, the airline continues to refine its service and introduce innovative programs.

Recognizing that food is an important part of the authentic Caribbean experience, the airline's meals are all designed, created and prepared under the supervision of Chef Louis Bailey, the world's only "Flying Chef." Meals feature traditional island dishes such as jerk pork, ackee and saltfish and a selection of international entrées.

Air Jamaica's first-class service is now known as "Top Class." Designed to offer passengers the ultimate in luxury and comfort, Top Class features upgraded in-flight meals and an affordable instant airport upgrade program.

Proving to be very popular with guests is Air Jamaica's exclusive beachside check-in, which is available at select hotels on Jamaica. Beachside check-in means that passengers can check their baggage and receive boarding passes right at their hotel, so they can spend more time on the beach rather than wait on lines at the airport.

And, spending time on the beach is easier than ever, thanks to Air Jamaica's "Island Hopping" program. Air Jamaica is the only carrier that makes it possible to visit two Caribbean islands for the price of one. Using Montego Bay as the hub, passengers booked for another destination can enjoy a complimentary stop-over on Jamaica or any of the other destinations served by the carrier. Additionally, for travelers looking for a lengthier travel experience that encompasses a broader range of Caribbean destinations, Air Jamaica has instituted the "Caribbean Hopper" fare, which allows those who travel to Jamaica to continue on to visit as many islands serviced by the airline as they would like, for one low price.

Air Jamaica prides itself on being one of the most service-oriented companies in the hospitality industry and it has a roster of

Air Jamaica has been named the "Best Airline to the Caribbean" at the World Travel Awards for the sixth consecutive year.

accolades to prove it. Air Jamaica has been named the "Best Airline to the Caribbean" at the World Travel Awards for the sixth consecutive year; has won the prestigious Five Star Diamond Award given by the American Academy of Hospitality Sciences; has been honored with the 2000 Sapphire Award for "Outstanding Food Service" from *Onboard Services Magazine*; and has been awarded the coveted "World's Best Honeymoon Airline" by *Modern Bride* magazine for three years.

Booking your travel to the Caribbean aboard Air Jamaica is "no problem" with Air Jamaica Vacations, one of the top U.S. vacation companies to the Caribbean. Whether traveling alone, as a couple, with a family, or with a business group, Air Jamaica Vacations offers a wide variety of air and hotel packages. Featured are world-class all-inclusive resorts, moderately priced hotels, intimate inns, fabulous villas, and unique properties on ten Caribbean destination islands.

Air Jamaica Vacations prides itself on delivering the finest vacation service at every level. Passengers flying to the Caribbean are treated to red carpet service on Air Jamaica's

nonstop champagne flights to Montego Bay, Jamaica, from twelve U.S. gateways, including Atlanta, Baltimore, Boston, Chicago, Fort Lauderdale, Houston, Los Angeles, Miami, Newark, JFK/New York, Orlando, and Philadelphia. Other major U.S. cities are accessible through connections with Air Jamaica's codeshare partner, Delta Air Lines.

At Air Jamaica's hub in Montego Bay, passengers find convenient jet-to-jet connections to Antigua, the Bahamas, Barbados, Bonaire, Curaçao, Grand Caymen, Grenada, and St. Lucia. Air Jamaica Express offers connecting service to the Turks and Caicos Islands.

Air Jamaica Vacations stays with vacationers all the way when they purchase a vacation package. Whether guests want to visit a breathtaking waterfall, horseback ride on the beach, explore underground caves, or swim with dolphins, Air Jamaica Vacations' on-island customer care representatives are just a phone call away.

8

Better In
The Bahamas

I WAS BOTH HAPPY AND PLEASED AS
PRIME MINISTER OF THE BAHAMAS TO
WOO AND THEN WELCOME BUTCH STEW-
ART AND SANDALS TO THE BAHAMAS'
HOTEL AND TOURISM SECTOR.

Rt. Hon. Hubert A. Ingraham
Former Prime Minister of The Bahamas

Deep-sea fishing off the coast of the islands of the Bahamas is angler heaven. Here, where the ocean ranges from transparent blue to turquoise, the sea is teeming with gamefish—wahoo, kingfish and tuna. There are also miles of shallow waters for bonefishing in this region, regarded as one of the world's premier sportfishing destinations. Some come for the pure thrill of reeling in their first ten-foot blue marlin. Others head to Abaco for a day of tangling with bonefish in knee-deep flats.

But fishing in the Bahamas is not only limited to fish. A good catch can be found on dry land, too.

Conditions became ideal for Sandals to cast its net in search of a Bahamian resort after 1992, when the Free National Movement won the elections in these islands. At the time, the newly elected prime minister, the Right Honourable Hubert Ingraham, sought to aggressively expand the Bahamas tourism sector. Government-owned hotels were divested and the recently named director-general of tourism, Vincent Vanderpool Wallace, initiated cutting-edge marketing strategies. When South African resort and casino developer Sol Kerzner of Sun International Resorts decided to invest in Paradise Island in 1993, Bahamas tourism got the boost it needed. Kerzner purchased the Paradise Island Hotel and Casino and converted it to an aquatic-themed casino-resort-entertainment complex named Atlantis Resort & Casino.

The time was ripe for Sandals to make its move in 1995. The bait was set, the line cast and Sandals reeled in a beauty: Le Meridien Royal Bahamian. The resort was originally built by Englishman Sir Oliver Simmons and opened on Christmas Day as the Balmoral Club, an elegant playground for royalty and celebrities such as the Prince of Wales and the Beatles.

In 1984, the thirteen-acre resort set along Cable Beach, also known as the "Bahamian Riviera," became part of the Wyndham Hotels group until 1990. From then on, Meridien Hotels managed the 145-room, twenty-seven-villa resort.

"I had my eyes on this place for a long time," said Stewart at the time. "And when I had the chance to buy it, I did. The addition of the Sandals Royal Bahamian to our portfolio will help us to become a major player in the tourism renaissance now taking place in the Bahamas."

HOTEL MAGNATES
Opposite: Former Bahamian Prime Minister Hubert Ingraham, far left, is pleased to have Butch Stewart and Sun International Chairman Sol Kerzner, right, as hoteliers in the Bahamas.

Majestic Tours

Tour Time

When guests visiting Nassau want a proper tour through the capital city, or wish to have a thrilling undersea encounter with a dolphin, or want to relish a day of sailing the open seas on a yacht, they typically call Majestic Tours, the premier operator of specialty tours and transportation in the Commonwealth of the Bahamas.

"We've had the privilege of working with Sandals and providing tours and transfers for its guests since Sandals Royal Bahamian first opened," says William A. Saunders, the dynamic president of Majestic Tours. Saunders is someone who knows the business. He's been a tourism practitioner for more than forty-five years, and has received numerous awards, including the Bahamas National Tourism Award.

Majestic Tours is well-versed and welcoming when it comes to touring in the Bahamas.

"We salute Butch Stewart for his entrepreneurship in our region and beyond."

WILLIAM A. SAUNDERS
PRESIDENT

Sandals' tenth resort promised to be its
best and most luxurious.

After Sandals purchased Le Meridien in May 1995, the resort was closed for a major refurbishing. Stephen Ziadie, one of Sandals' long-time general managers, was selected to be general manager.

"Mr. Stewart visualized this hotel as the jewel in the Sandals crown," says Ziadie.

Come Sail Away

In 1996, Rapsody Cruises, operator of Dreamer Catamarans, was offered the opportunity to dock at Sandals Montego Bay and provide sailing and snorkeling tours to Sandals' guests at all three Montego Bay resorts. Soon, *Tropical Dreamer*, a 53-foot Gold Coast yacht, sailed in, and the fun has been going strong ever since.

The three-hour adventure aboard the Dreamer boats begins at Sandals Montego Bay and continues within the Montego Bay Marine Park. Dreamer catamarans provide everything guests need for a memorable day of sailing and snorkeling replete with a snorkeling guide who offers instruction and first-class equipment. The ship's forward stairway lowers into the water, providing easy access for swimming and snorkeling.

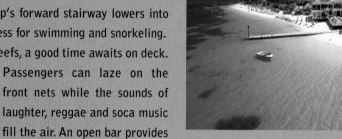

After exploring the coral reefs, a good time awaits on deck. Passengers can laze on the front nets while the sounds of laughter, reggae and soca music fill the air. An open bar provides thirst-quenching libations. And a soothing foot massage might be in order to warm up the toes before learning the latest dance moves from the fun-loving crew.

Tropical Dreamer has proved so popular with Sandals guests that another 53-foot Gold Coast yacht, *Day Dreamer*, designed for the ultimate sailing experience, has been added to the fleet.

"We love working with the Sandals team. They display a professionalism that is unequaled and makes our job easy."

GREG LEE
CAPTAIN

Bottom photo: Sandals Resorts International

A ROYAL RESORT

Sandals spruced up the architecture, which was already quite striking. Reminiscent of Greece and of seventeenth-century Versailles, Corinthian, Ionic and Doric columns were used throughout the pink-and-white structures on the property.

"Everyone scouted for details and ideas that would set the property apart and give it a sophisticated edge," recalls Ziadie. "A few months before we opened, Mr. Stewart was in England, where he visited an authentic pub. He decided that a pub would make a great addition to the resort. He was able to purchase and dismantle antique pub pieces from all over the U.K., which arrived one day in a forty-foot container. We carved out a space, which was originally intended as a meeting venue, hired a company from the U.K., and re-created an authentic pub within three weeks!"

Indeed, every few weeks shipments of some sort or another arrived at the property. Inside the crates were incredible Romanesque statues, enormous crystal chandeliers and magnificent antique pieces.

TOUR TIME
Former Bahamian Prime Minister Hubert Ingraham, flanked by Stewart, right, and hotel General Manager Stephen Ziadie tour the grounds.

Thirteen months of work ensued. The construction crew stripped down the resort and rebuilt it from the ground up. When the resort reopened as Sandals Royal Bahamian Resort & Spa in June 1996, it was a stunner, with six restaurants, four swimming pools, a sports complex, a new European-style spa and a twenty-five acre semiprivate island a half mile from the property.

"We've just gone overboard to test the waters and see if something this luxurious can succeed in the market," Stewart said at the time.

awards and accolades

Within a year of opening, Sandals Royal Bahamian Resort & Spa received the coveted AAA Four Diamond rating. And, the hotel's new spa concept also received accolades: The readers of *Condé Nast Traveler* voted the Signature Spa at the Royal Bahamian the "Top Caribbean Spa Resort" after its first year of operation.

"Butch promised to take a poorly managed government-owned and -operated jewel of a hotel, the Balmoral Beach, off the hands of the Hotel Corporation of The Bahamas and to transform it into an upscale, all-inclusive hotel and spa," says Hubert Ingraham, former prime minister of the Bahamas. "He was as good as his word. Expending considerably more than the sums originally committed for the project, he renovated and rejuvenated the hotel and it reopened to rave reviews. Recognition by the tourism industry, which bestowed numerous accolades, is most deserved. Butch Stewart is a model Caribbean man. He has put his money where his mouth is ... in the Caribbean."

Founded in 1991, Pevonia headquarters in Daytona Beach, Florida, operates with great success under the leader- ship of Philippe and Sylvie Hennessy.

Sandals and Pevonia partner to deliver guests the most relaxing and rejuvenating spa, face and body treatment experience.

Ahh, Spa

When the Sandals team first began exploring the possibility of offering a spa experience at its new resort in Nassau, the group knew that choosing a committed high-caliber partner for treatment and skincare products was an important part of its success. Karen Sprung, group spa and fitness director for Sandals Resorts International, headed the challenge of selecting a new skincare line. She was determined to choose a company with an excellent reputation, superior products and first-rate training, and she soon began the search.

Coincidentally, just days later, Philippe Hennessy, the president of Pevonia International, one of the top skincare companies in the world, stopped in at Sandals Royal Bahamian to request a property tour. Hennessy was on a long-awaited vacation with his wife, Sylvie, the creator and founder of Pevonia, and their family.

Hennessy fondly recalls: "I remember worrying that I was ruining Sylvie's vacation. We were finally in the Bahamas on our family vacation and I insisted that we visit this new resort. I was truly touched by the gracious reception of Mr. Stephen Ziadie, the hotel's general manager, never expecting that he would take the time to see me without an appointment. But before I knew it, I was given a tour, and my family and I were generously invited to enjoy a day of leisure at the resort. From

the start, the relationship between Sandals and Pevonia was founded on courtesy, professionalism and mutual respect. This continues to be the case today, nearly a decade later."

Shortly after the initial meeting between Hennessy and Ziadie, the Pevonia and Sandals teams got together to explore the possibility of working together. Sandals then selected Pevonia Botanica as the skincare line of choice for the Royal Bahamian as well as for all future Sandals resorts.

Pevonia Botanica was chosen because of its philosophy and quality, and the visible results of its products. The line offers holistic botanical products and treatments that nurture, rejuvenate and restore skin's natural beauty. And the product formulations are continually updated to incorporate breakthrough scientific treatment techniques. Another of its marks of distinction is Pevonia's spa portfolio, which boasts some of the most exclusive and prestigious destination spas and day spas worldwide.

The extensive line of Pevonia Botanica products includes more than one hundred and fifty specialized products and fifty professional face and body spa treatments, which are continuously updated. The entire line of skin, body and spa care products and treatments are environmentally conscious, not tested on animals and non-comedogenic.

Founded in 1991, Pevonia headquarters in Daytona Beach, Florida, operates with great success under the leadership of Philippe and Sylvie

Pevonia Botanica was chosen because of its philosophy and quality, and the visible results of its products.

Hennessy. Internationally regarded as the force responsible for the development and creation of Pevonia Botanica skin, body and spa care, Philippe and Sylvie provide an impressive accumulation of expertise, knowledge and dedication toward the advancement of aesthetics.

"The guest experience has always been Sandals' number one priority. As such, it's important that our guests receive only the finest skincare treatments and personal care products available," explains Sandals' Sprung. "Not only is Pevonia an outstanding product, but the array of professional treatments, the level of service, the caliber of training, and the stellar support we receive from Pevonia is incredible."

Working together, Sandals' spa team and Pevonia Botanica have created a spa sanctuary where guests can escape and indulge in holistic care. The spa experience has become an integral—and growing—part of the Sandals and Beaches vacation. "The number of spas in the Sandals chain has increased rapidly," Sprung points out. Sandals currently operates more than a dozen spas, with several more spa projects under development.

"Pevonia products are a big hit with our guests," continues Sprung. "And the caliber of the Pevonia team truly elevates the brand. Pevonia has enabled the progression of our spas to their current level of success. The folks at Pevonia are always transferring their knowledge and positive energy to our spa team members. Knowing that the products deliver outstanding results gives us a sense of pride through association as we greet our resort guests and perform treatment services."

The spas at Sandals offer a rejuvenating, romantic escape with enticing hot and cold plunge pools surrounded by lush green and fuchsia landscaping.

RETREAT

The advent of Sandals Signature Spa at Sandals Royal Bahamian was no random coincidence, rather another example of how the resort group continues to give vacationers what they want when they want it. In the early 1990s, baby boomers had started to embrace the growing health and fitness phenomenon in large numbers. Exercise classes were becoming more structured, equipment was getting sophisticated. Johnny G. trademarked Spinning® in 1992, and companies like Reebok dominated the aerobics market with new trends like the step and the slide.

"And we kept in step with the marketplace—we recognized the importance of raising the fitness level at the properties," says Karen Sprung. Having joined the Sandals family in 1981 as a Playmaker, Sprung worked her way up and is now group spa and fitness director for Sandals Resorts International.

"By the mid-1990s, people's lifestyles were changing," adds Sprung. "With the pace of life getting faster and, often, married couples both working outside the home, we found that vacationers were desperately seeking a balance between activity and relaxation."

Yoga, massage therapy, facials, and the notion of pampering oneself were coming into their own. Spas were growing rapidly and were becoming increasingly popular. In fact, a new trend in vacation travel was taking place: the getaway for unwinding from the stresses of everyday life. And the Caribbean, with its languid landscape, was a natural fit for renewing body, mind and spirit.

The Caribbean is a natural fit for renewing body, mind and spirit.

"We put ourselves in the mind-set of the guest when it came time to set up the spa program," Sprung says. "Our feeling was that the spa should become an oasis, an area of the resort where guests would feel like they just had to be."

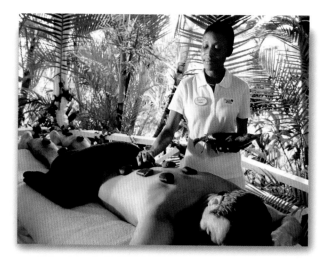

Indeed, with European estheticians on hand to train local spa personnel, and Pevonia products from Switzerland used at all the Signature spas, Sandals' guests came seeking sanctuary, and a treatment or two, at the spa.

The spa treatments are designed to work in harmony with the tropics. "One very popular treatment is the Sunrise Sea and Scrub," explains Sprung. "We take guests down to the pier where we crush almonds from the almond tree, mix the almonds with a salt scrub and massage the mixture into the skin as a body exfoliant. After the treatment, guests jump into the sea, which acts like a tonic. It's a one-of-a-kind experience that they can't get in any other destination."

STONE AGE
Hot stone massage is just one of the many luxurious spa treatments that await guests at Sandals and Beaches resorts.

Nassau Paradise Island Promotion Board

Paradise Found

It's easy to see why the Sandals team in the mid-'90s fell in love with Nassau and Paradise Island, in the Bahamas, and why couples continue flocking to the capital city: Not only is the location spectacular, but this popular destination packs a powerful vacation combination, mixing international appeal with tropical ease.

"As we say in the Bahamas, 'It just keeps getting better,'" says Obie Wilchcombe, Minister of Tourism for the Bahamas. "When Sandals finally graced our shores in 1996, with Sandals Royal Bahamian, a world-class luxury resort, it really raised our profile. We're thrilled to have them as one of the stylish resorts in our Nassau and Paradise Island destination."

Sandy beaches. Vibrant nightlife. Colonial charm. Tropical beauty. Add to that a romantic, world-class, award-winning luxury resort for couples only. What's not to love in Nassau and on Paradise Island?

Nassau and Paradise Island is an idyllic destination for those seeking a playful getaway.

Treatment venues can be tailored for personal preference.

In late 2004, Sandals unveiled Red Lane™ Spa, a new spa concept designed to offer vacationers a truly memorable destination spa experience. Available at Sandals and Beaches properties, the collection of indulgent retreats provides guests with premium pampering and exclusive treatments. "We are constantly seeking ways to provide our guests with a higher level of services and amenities," says Karen Sprung. "With the launch of this concept, we are offering a second-to-none experience that will attract and exceed the expectations of the most discerning spa connoisseur from across the globe. The reinterpretation of our spas is one more example of how we continue to reinvent the vacation experience and make it better."

The luxurious spas combine fine European traditions with characteristic Caribbean flair, all in settings replete with imported marble, classic mahogany millwork and original art. Treatments are formulated and custom-mixed with vitamin-rich island fruits like red oranges and grapefruit, and organic seaweed, local honey and almonds and an assortment of other tropical delicacies. One of several signature treatments, Wake Up and Smell the Coffee, takes on a whole new meaning at the Red Lane Spas. Inspired by Jamaica's indigenous Blue Mountain coffee beans, the intoxicating treatment begins with a gentle skin exfoliation followed by a coffee wrap and warm milk bath. A relaxing aromatherapy massage using coffee-infused oils comes next, and the finishing touch is a freshly brewed cup of Blue Mountain coffee to drink. Other signature offerings include a Seaside Exfoliation using red almonds and local honey, a Signature Lemongrass Body Scrub with an infusion of herbs and ginseng, and an Ortanique Orange Scrub, which incorporates exotic tropical sweet oranges and natural brown sugar.

Recognizing that each individual is the architect of his or her own vitality and well-being, Red Lane Spas offer an array of treatments designed to cater to its clientele. "We present spa menus that provide a range of options, from romantic treatments designed for couples, to other specialized treatments for children and teens," adds Sprung. Even treatment venues can be tailored for personal preference, from the beach and garden gazebo to in-room indulgences.

Today, the spa business at Sandals spreads as smoothly as the massage oil.

PAMPERING YOUR WAY
Whether on the beach or under a gazebo, a relaxing massage or facial is just one of many memorable Red Lane Spa experiences.

The Bahamas

Not only has Burns House been successful in business, it also is the country's leading corporate citizen.

The next time you're in the Bahamas drinking a cold Kalik or Guinness beer or strolling past a liquor store, remember this inspiring story about Garet "Tiger" Finlayson, a local boy from Andros, the largest of the Bahamian islands. He became the most successful black entrepreneur in the history of the Bahamas.

Finlayson's working life began early. At age fifteen, after completion of a six-month course at the Teachers Training College in Nassau, Finlayson returned to Andros to teach at an all-age school. After his career in teaching, he took up tailoring in his step-father's shop, where he became one of the best tailors of his era. A few years later, in order to make more money, Finlayson decided to become a waiter and bartender.

Means Business

his sales manager," says Finlayson. "We gave our biggest competitor quite a stir for that first year or two. Then we were bought out by the competitor in 1970 and I became sales manager of that competitor's company, and my boss became the general manager."

Eventually Finlayson went on to become general manager, and within two years, ironically, Finlayson ended up acquiring the General Bahamian Company, which is the company that sold him the furniture business.

Never one to rest on his laurels, Finlayson expanded his business by purchasing an airline catering firm, Nassau Caterers; a hotel on Nassau's West Bay Street; a night club; a restaurant; an automobile dealership; and a chain of pharmacies.

In 1987, in partnership with brewing giant Heineken, Finlayson opened the Commonwealth Brewery. And, in March 2000, he purchased Butler & Sands Limited, a leading Bahamas beer, wine and spirits merchant.

Burns House is the exclusive distributor for Kalik, Kalik Light, Kalik Gold, Heineken, Vitamalt, and Guinness. It also maintains sole distributor rights for Anheuser-Busch and for Gilbey's, the number one gin in the Bahamas. In addition, the company is a major player in the wine market, offering Gallo, Chapoutier, Bolla, Piat, Zimmerman, Taittinger, and Joseph Drouhin.

Not only is Burns House successful in business, it also is the Bahamas' leading corporate citizen, donating to hundreds of charities and sponsoring numerous musical, sporting and cultural events throughout the Bahamas.

"We are a firm believer in contributing to the growth and development of our community," says Finlayson. Putting words into action, Finlayson, who owns the three main liquor store chains in the Bahamas, is seeking to franchise out all eighty-eight stores in an attempt to encourage and empower locals to use their skills to better themselves.

Garet "Tiger" Finlayson

"These people really deserve a chance," says Finlayson, "and I want to help make it happen for them."

Making it happen is obviously something that Finlayson does well.

No ordinary waiter, he negotiated a deal with his boss to earn a commission on each drink he sold.

Having polished his selling skills as a server, Finlayson took a job as a car salesman for Island Motors. Here is where he met his mark, regularly selling four or five more vehicles than the other salesmen. Then one day, Finlayson made a sale that would set him on a course for future success. An overly cautious customer had been thinking about making a new car purchase—thinking for more than four years! None of the salesmen at the car showroom had been able to convince him to buy a car. But Finlayson did. The customer's boss was so impressed that he offered Finlayson a job at his office furniture business.

"I took it up and ran the business with him, eventually becoming

Community
Works

IF YOU ARE OPERATING A BUSINESS
IN A LOCAL COMMUNITY, THEN YOU
MUST EMBRACE THAT COMMUNITY
AND EMBRACE IT WELL.

Leo Lambert
Corporate Communications Director
Sandals Resorts International

Extending beyond property boundaries, the Sandals Resorts team is fully involved in supporting local communities with projects that make a difference. The concept of giving back was embedded in the company culture from the start.

Students from the
St. Christopher School for
the Deaf, in St. Ann,
Jamaica, pictured at right,
participate in a workshop
organized by Sandals
Dunn's River Golf Resort
& Spa.

A student from the Children's
Emergency Hostel in the
Bahamas, pictured below,
is outfitted with a backpack
and new school supplies,
compliments of Sandals
Royal Bahamian Resort & Spa.

Young cricket players
from St. Lucia, pictured
above, get tips from their
hero, Gordon Greenidge,
during a cricket clinic
hosted by Sandals Halcyon
Beach St. Lucia.

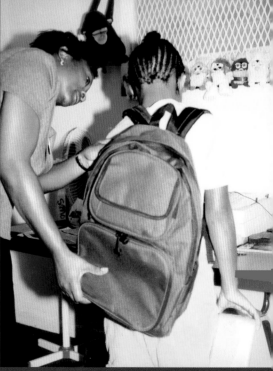

CREATING A CULTURE

"We do not view ourselves as a charity organization," says Leo Lambert, corporate communications director for Sandals Resorts International. "We believe we can direct people to solutions and are here to offer leadership to the communities in which we operate. It's important to understand that we don't just write a check, throw money and disappear. We truly get involved in understanding what the needs are and in supplying necessary materials to fill voids."

Through community outreach, Sandals has brought about a hospitality culture, important in countries where tourism is a mainstay of the economy. "We let people in the community know how the hotel business works and why it's important to deliver quality service," says Lambert. "It's good for the community and good for business all around. You see, the product we're putting out must operate at international standards. Therefore, everybody's attitude towards service has to be top-notch."

The thrust of Sandals' community outreach efforts is focused on education, youth development and health.

Sandals team members in St. Lucia, pictured at left, lend their time to help paint a local school.

They all Jump
up 1 2 3

Good listeners
My
My
My
My
My

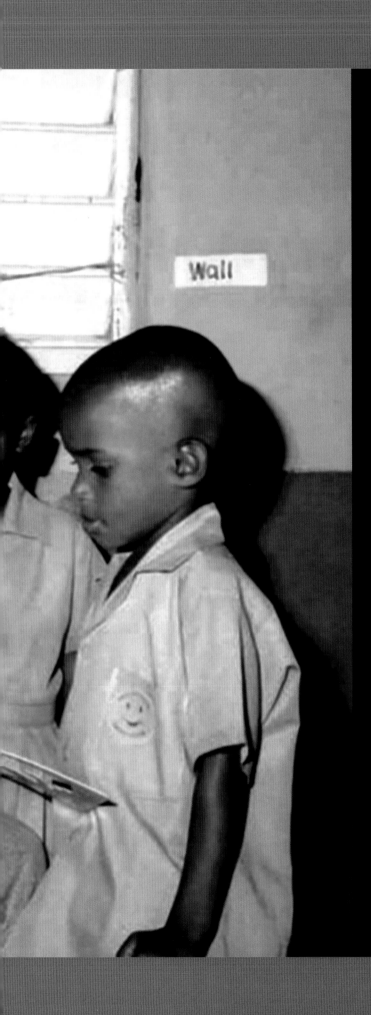

WELL-SCHOOLED

Schools are a critical area of support for Sandals. "Students who are now in school are the very people that we are going to employ in a few years," says Lambert. "And we have a policy of employing as many people as we can from our host communities."

Through Sandals' Adopt-A-School program, each Sandals and Beaches resort is required to take under its wing at least one school in its community, based on proximity and need.

"When we approached the management at Sandals Negril in the mid-nineteen eighties seeking assistance, there was no hesitation on their part," says Melrose Myrie, principal of Whitehall Basic & Preparatory School in Negril, Jamaica. "We've worked closely with them ever since. The Sandals team assists with the maintenance of the building, provides computers and organizes programs for our students and teachers."

Describing the program, Merrick Fray, managing director for Sandals Resorts International, says, "Sandals team members meet with the principal and teachers and ask, 'What is it that we can do to assist you in these areas?' For example, if a school needs help with its mathematics program, Sandals will supply workbooks, videos and other material to bring that program up to speed. Or if students are particularly skilled in music, arts or athletics, Sandals works with teachers and coaches to help develop those skills. In other words, we provide schools with the necessary tools."

"If you ask, most hotels will give you a donation," adds Carolyn Archibald, principal of the Dunnottar School in Castries, St. Lucia. "Not only does Sandals donate, but they arrive en masse! When they provide lunch, for example, the chef and senior managers arrive and serve it. They spend time getting to know the students and take the time to show they care."

Sandals General Manager Merelene Warner, pictured below, congratulates students at the Annual Creative Arts Competition, which promotes talent among youth.

Students from the St. Lucia School for the Deaf, pictured at right, perform a song during their visit to Sandals Grande St. Lucia Spa & Golf Resort.

Above: Leo Lambert, corporate communications director for Sandals Resorts International, far left, and Franklyn Eaton, general manager, present computers and books to the principal of St. Lucia's Balata Primary School.

MAKING THEIR MARK

In 1997, the company initiated Sandals Community Scholarship Awards, making a commitment to children who show great promise but whose families may not have the financial means to assist them with their continuing education. "We take students through high school by paying for tuition, books and the like, provided they maintain certain standards," says Lambert. "There are now seventy-seven young students who would have otherwise missed out on an opportunity to attend high school. We're going to be sure that they make their mark on society."

Says scholarship recipient Satalda Sterling, "When I passed my common entrance exam, my mom was happy for me, but I knew she wondered where she would get the money so I could continue my education. I am grateful to Sandals Inn for providing me with a scholarship and support throughout my years at Mount Alvernia High School. Sandals continues to inspire students like me by granting scholarships to those in need."

Duke Mouton, another student receiving a boost up, says, "As a scholarship recipient of Sandals Ocho Rios, I have been given the opportunity to receive a proper education. I consider the program as one of the great successes of our time."

Tourism in Schools is yet another innovative Sandals community program whereby students learn how tourism ultimately benefits them and their families. Hotel managers visit schools and speak with students about how tourism works, from the perspective of a house-keeping manager or an executive chef. "We're shaping how these students think about tourism and teaching them the impact it has on the economy," says Lambert. "It's all about creating a mind-set and helping to contribute to nation building in our own unique way."

"If you don't share, then you aren't serving

a purpose."

— BUTCH STEWART

REACHING OUT

Sandals works hard at deepening its partnerships in host communities. In 1995, the chain struck a deal with the Rural Agricultural Development Authority (RADA): Sandals provides local farmers with seeds for select crops that can be grown in the Caribbean; RADA provides the extension services to make sure the project works.

"By supporting our local farmers, we get more fresh produce grown locally and can provide the freshest food to our guests," says Lambert. "In turn, we offer a guaranteed market to the farmers, changing their business approach. In a sense it's remarkable what we're doing. We're creating successful businesses for farmers. The program was so well received that we've had to extend it."

RADA agrees. "There's a wonderful synergy at play here," says Janet Lawrence, RADA project manager. "All parties, from the government, hotel sector and farmers, are working hard in tandem to make sure the venture is a success. I think that this program is breaking in a different culture by training our farmers to work together and become managers of their own businesses. The farmers are just beginning to see their farming enterprise as a business."

IN GOOD HEALTH

Every month, almost all Sandals and Beaches resorts provide local health facilities with assistance in terms of supplies and services. "It's not superficial," states Lambert. "It's actually reminding these people that someone cares. These are people that have contributed to our society in some way and now, because they are sick or elderly, need someone to assist them. We read to them, talk to them, listen to their concerns, and provide health clinics."

Sandals Dunn's River Golf Resort & Spa is particularly active in providing health care to remote communities. "Health-care initiatives are my pet project," says Lyndsay Isaacs, the hotel's longtime public relations manager. "We've developed a collaborative team of doctors and nurses and a pharmaceutical company to provide free medical and dental checkups and medications to the local rural community."

Doctor David Lambert adds, "It is very rewarding for me to offer volunteer services to the wider community, especially where the need is great. I commend Sandals for its role in upgrading the lives of so many."

"Working with Sandals on health-related matters for the rural community has been one of the most enlightening periods of our medical career," concur doctors Alisha Danielle Robb and Geoffrey Walcott. "The experience has been tremendous and has provided us with the opportunity to serve for the greater good."

As Sandals continues to grow throughout the Caribbean, it has used its resources well, sparking the potential of youth and providing for those in need. "We hope to make a real difference by changing lives and transforming communities," says Merrick Fray, managing director for Sandals Resorts International.

10 Going Green

BEACHES NEGRIL, WITH ITS ENVIRON-
MENTALLY CONSCIOUS PERSPECTIVE,
WAS A CATALYST FOR THE HOTEL
GROUP TO PUT EVEN MORE EMPHASIS
ON CONSERVATION.

At Long Bay in Negril, Jamaica, twenty acres of verdant wooded land front the shoreline. Thirty-foot-high palms and guango trees thrive in this mangrove swamp. When Real Resorts, a consortium of Jamaican and international investors, purchased the site, protecting the natural flora and fauna was of the utmost importance. Led by Jamaican businessman and chairman of Real Resorts, O.K. Melhado, the group sought to partner with a leading hotelier to develop a resort and operate it.

They turned to Sandals and struck a deal.

A NEW RESORT FOR THE SOUTH COAST: "Beaches" is the name of the Sandals resort to be built on Jamaica's South Coast by Mr. Gordon 'Butch' Stewart. He described the facility as "the most ambitious holiday resort in the Caribbean to date." According to Mr. Stewart, he hopes it will be the first of something big for the area. Here Mr. Stewart displays the name and logo at a recent press conference to update the media on plans for the resort. He is being assisted by Dr. George Phillip, Group Co-ordinator for the ATL Group of Companies.

PROTECTED PROPERTY

Given the location, with its environmental sensitivity, an impact assessment was conducted before construction began. Based on the study, a decision was made to leave much of the existing natural setting intact and build around it. Surveys were undertaken to locate the larger trees on property and construct buildings around them.

Longtime Sandals architect Evan Williams oversaw the design: "We were very environmentally conscious while handling this project. In terms of the architecture, we chose to use a lot of wood rather than concrete. Not only did we consider the physical facility, but also our surroundings. A detailed landscape and vegetation protection plan was developed to preserve large sections of the natural forest. Many of the larger trees were left in place and we built a ten-acre nursery across the street to temporarily house the rest. We transplanted about five thousand indigenous plants, which allowed us to save almost ninety percent of the landscaping."

In fact, the Negril property was the first in Jamaica to incorporate environmental protection measures from the early design stages through to completion. "The approach was initiated by our own project team and was entirely voluntary," adds O.K. Melhado.

Large areas of swampy vegetation were also left intact for nesting crabs and turtles, which come there to lay their eggs during certain times of the year. Members of the Sandals staff assisted hatchlings in their journey from land to sea by strategically laying bamboo pipes on the property for the turtles and crabs to crawl through.

"A detailed landscape plan was developed to preserve large sections of the natural forest."

A Rousing Ride

Inspired by Maui's bike ride down a dormant volcano, Gregory Naldrett and his partners, Dr. Thomas DeVaughn and Althea Bryan, sought to re-create the experience on Jamaica. In 1991, they found an eighteen-mile stretch of road located five thousand feet high in the island's Blue Mountains. "We worked hard to get the road into shape," says Naldrett. "Today it's one of the best paved roads on Jamaica, and definitely the most scenic."

About ten thousand visitors each year hop on bikes and cycle away with Blue Mountain Bicycle Tours, giving them an eco-friendly, up close and personal journey through the Blue Mountains. Surrounded by the lush countryside, bicyclists coast down the mountain past rain forests, rivers, waterfalls, and coffee plantations. The tour includes a stop at picturesque Blue Mountain Café, an open-air restaurant where an authentic Jamaican brunch and lunch are served.

"We immerse guests into the history and culture of the island, giving them a true glimpse into rural Jamaica," says DeVaughn. "They discover interesting facts about Jamaica and hear the local dialect spoken. Along the way, travelers pass by manicured acres of coffee crops, which yield the island's coveted Blue Mountain coffee. Our rest stop is on the site of a 150-year-old payout station where farmers once brought their coffee so they wouldn't have to travel all the way to Kingston." It is fitting that a century and a half later, Blue Mountain coffee is still offered on the original site.

History. Beauty. Culture. This memorable bike tour will definitely leave riders content.

> "We fit hand in glove with the Sandals concept of providing a true Jamaican experience."
>
> ALTHEA S. BRYAN
> MANAGING DIRECTOR

Butch Stewart is passionate about trees. Those who know him are familiar with his refrain, "You don't cut down a tree." Here, in the words of Sandals team members, are insights and anecdotes to elaborate on the connection between the Sandals chairman and trees.

He has a love for gardens and color, and an almost reverence for trees. His attitude is that a tree takes years to reach its full size, so don't dare think you can just cut it down.

**ELEANOR MILLER
PROJECTS DIRECTOR**

If you want to get a good cussing, just go and cut down a bougainvillea tree, or any other tree for that matter. Trust me, he knows every tree on every property!

**BALDWIN POWELL
GENERAL MANAGER**

Mr. Stewart is an outdoorsman. He believes that by removing a tree, in a sense, you're destroying a part of the environment. It's appealing to have original trees on property and he does everything possible to preserve them.

**JEFF MCKITTY
GENERAL MANAGER**

We couldn't get enough sunlight on one of the buildings at Sandals Negril because of bamboo growing nearby. The surveyor suggested we chop it out. I learned very quickly that you don't chop down anything green without asking Mr. Stewart's permission . . . not that you'll be getting the permission anyway.

**LARRY MCDONALD
GROUP DIRECTOR OF
ENGINEERING**

A RESORT FOR EVERYONE

The original thought was to develop the property at Long Bay into another successful Sandals couples-only resort. By early 1995, concepts evolved, plans were set, renderings were drawn, and construction was under way for the $32 million property. Then came a switch. Rather than develop a couples-only resort, a decision was made to branch out in a new direction.

The official ground-breaking ceremony took place in May 1995. One and a half years later, in early February 1997, Sandals introduced its first family resort when Beaches Negril opened its doors. Beaches Negril became the first all-inclusive Sandals resort to welcome singles and families, and couples.

The resort looked as if it had always been there, largely due to the mature foliage and aesthetic design. With its use of cedarwood, coral stone and red tiles and its open-air design, Beaches Negril had a gracious, natural feel.

"We had a truly unique opportunity to incorporate the synthesis of the Sandals experience when designing the property," says architect Evan Williams. "Sandals is, of course, uniquely Caribbean. That heritage easily translated to Beaches Negril. We took all the major colonial and other styles that helped shape the region—Spanish Colonial, English Georgian, West Indian, Chinese and Arawak—and added those into the design."

PRIME CELEBRATION
**Jamaica Prime Minister
P.J. Patterson, right, and O.K.
Melhado, middle, an investor in
Beaches Negril, are on hand for
the ground-breaking ceremony.**

Beaches: Resorts for Everyone

The Beaches brand, marketed as part of the Sandals family, has proved to be a welcome relation. Launching into the family market in 1997 with Beaches Negril, the brand was a natural extension for Sandals—after all, the Sandals resort group had been wildly popular with couples for fifteen years before Beaches Negril opened its doors. "More and more, we heard people say they'd love to come to Sandals but they couldn't because they had kids, or they were single parents or grandparents," says Merrick Fray, managing director for Sandals Resorts International. "We wanted to create a resort that had the qualities of Sandals but would give children of any age an enjoyable vacation experience."

Today, the Beaches family has flourished, with its own next of kin. Three Beaches resorts dot the Jamaican coastline, while the Turks and Caicos Islands also boasts a Beaches resort.

With exceptional programs and action-packed activities for families, kids, single parents, groups, and, yes, couples, too, Beaches truly is the all-inclusive resort for everyone.

Beaches® is a proud sponsor of
see it on PBS Kids™
123 SESAME STREET

With a reputation in the industry for knowing how to run a family resort, Jeff McKitty was recruited by Sandals as general manager. "When I came to Sandals, I knew what had to be done to make it a family-friendly resort. We wanted a family resort that was better than anything at the time, and the idea was that everything that goes into Sandals had to go into Beaches, even though we were catering to a different market. So there were pools for adults, and for toddlers. Some restaurants catered to adults only, while others were created for family dining. We built a video games arcade and a nursery for the younger children. Staying sensitive to all guest needs was key. For example, many times we had three generations of family traveling together. We built ramps and constructed rooms and restaurants for people in wheelchairs and for parents with strollers in tow."

Besides blossoming into a successful brand in its own right, Beaches Negril, with its environment-conscious perspective, was a catalyst for Sandals to put even more emphasis on conservation. Eventually, the organization formalized its commitment to the environment by championing progressive green programs.

"We wanted a **family resort** that was **better** than anything at the time."

A Time to Travel

Island Savvy

When Sue Schmerling opened her Coral Springs, Florida travel agency, A Time to Travel, in 1997, she decided to specialize in the Caribbean. She traveled extensively to the islands, educating herself about the nuances of each destination.

Schmerling, who is also known as "Jamaica Sue" due to her expert knowledge of Jamaica, prides herself on getting to know her clients and attending to their travel needs. "In the Internet age, my clients appreciate the personalized service they receive when they book with me," she says.

A Time to Travel plans all-inclusive Caribbean vacations of all sorts, from weddings and honeymoons to reunions. Schmerling is certified as a "Best of the Best" Sandals Specialist. "To better serve my clients, I have made it my business to visit resorts and to get to know many of the general managers," says Schmerling.

Photo: Jamaica Tourist Board

"Jamaica will always be my home-away-from-home."

SUE SCHMERLING
OWNER

"BUTCH STEWART AND HIS ALL-INCLUSIVE RESORT GROUP, SANDALS, HAVE MADE A TREMENDOUS IMPACT ON TOURISM, BOTH FOR JAMAICA AND THE CARIBBEAN. OUR COUNTRY ENJOYS A RICH TRADITION IN THE HOSPITALITY INDUSTRY, AND THE FIRST-CLASS SANDALS CHAIN HAS ENHANCED OUR COUNTRY'S REPUTATION WORLDWIDE. BUTCH STEWART IS AN ENERGETIC AND INNOVATIVE ENTREPRENEUR WHO HAS ACHIEVED WELL-DESERVED SUCCESS."

Most Hon. P.J. Patterson
Prime Minister of Jamaica

"Our environmental awareness grew as we watched Beaches Negril constructed."

"While Sandals has always been environmentally friendly, we didn't have a formal program per se," says longtime Sandals General Manager Baldwin Powell. "As general manager of Sandals Negril in the early '90s, I, along with Wayne Cummings, the resident manager at the time, had some small programs in place. We got involved with the non-profit group Caribbean Alliance for Sustained Tourism and began utilizing water savers, energy lighting and the like. Our environmental awareness grew as we watched Beaches Negril constructed. Soon after, I became aware of Green Globe 21 and what some hotels were doing in terms of following environmental practices."

Green Globe 21 is a worldwide environmental management benchmarking and certification program for sustainable travel and tourism. It was launched by the World Travel & Tourism Council in 1994 as a means to ensure that hospitality organizations take the necessary measures to protect the environment. As facilitators, Green Globe helps to monitor the industry and sets standards for environmental, social and economic responsibility.

Supported by main industry and government organizations, Green Globe 21 was born out of Agenda 21 and the Principles for Sustainable Development endorsed by 182 governments at the United Nations Rio de Janeiro Earth Summit in 1992. In 1999, Green Globe 21 was established as an independent company and it now has six hundred members in one hundred countries and has certified nearly 150 travel operations.

HELPING HANDS
Local school children learn about nature from Sandals team members as they help nurture the environment.

> *"We have a strong heritage in the agriculture business on Jamaica. And we are dedicated to a philosophy of producing 'the' premium quality poultry, fish and beef in the Caribbean."*
>
> ROBERT LEVY
> PRESIDENT AND CEO
> OF THE GROUP OF COMPANIES

Quality

Getting their fill of fish, chicken and beef is "no problem" for guests of Sandals and Beaches resorts thanks to Jamaica Broilers Group Limited. Devotees of the South Beach or Atkins diet—and anyone else who simply appreciates a delicious roast chicken, fillet of fish or grilled steak—can rest assured that quality protein is prominently served for breakfast, lunch and dinner at all Sandals properties.

For more than forty years, Jamaica Broilers Group has been a proud supplier of poultry, fish and beef to international restaurant and hotel chains. The company has established and maintained a reputation for the highest-quality protein products. With strict internal procedures managed by a well-trained workforce, Jamaica

Counts

Broilers shows commitment to ensuring that all products deliver the quality specifications that are promised.

Experienced farmers tend to the chickens and millions of fertile eggs produced from the best breeds available worldwide. The farmers are supervised by skilled agricultural technicians and are supported by a nationwide service comprised of veterinary laboratory and nutritional facilities. With more than twenty-four million birds processed annually, Jamaica Broilers runs the largest processing plant in the Caribbean, and the Grade A birds it sells are known as "the best-dressed chickens."

A world pacesetter in farm fishing technology, Jamaica Broilers has modern, fully automated plants that harvest fish whole and fillet them in seconds.

Jamaica's prized fresh red tilapia, a culinary delight, is one of the most popular and tastiest fish it produces and is found on the menu at Sandals and Beaches resorts, often served jerked with a pineapple-mango salsa.

Beef is another innovative area for the Jamaica Broilers Group. The company is constantly exploring the development of new technology in agriculture and has perfected the bio-fermentation process whereby highly nutritional animal feed is produced. In its feedlot operations, cattle are reared on the best feeds, yielding a premium quality beef.

"We have a strong heritage in the agriculture business on Jamaica," says Robert Levy, president and CEO of the Group of Companies. "And we are dedicated to a philosophy of producing *the* premium quality poultry, fish and beef in the Caribbean. Our clients include Jamaica's finest hotels, restaurants and supermarkets, and we are very proud to provide them with an excellent array of tasty products."

IT'S NOT EASY BEING GREEN

"We researched the Green Globe program and realized that we were already incorporating a few of their standards," recalls Powell. "Our feeling was, let's continue down this path and formalize our program."

The process and systems that need to be certified by Green Globe 21 require a hotel's serious commitment to its environmental program, including establishing unwavering standards and developing a sustainable environmental management system. The obligation is not to be taken lightly.

"In order to get started, Green Globe needed to conduct an audit of the property," says Powell. "We approached Mr. Stewart about initiating the program at Sandals Negril and explained the level of commitment, resources and cost that would be involved, which was no small matter. After hearing our ideas, I clearly remember his response, 'You're pushing on an open door. Go with it, we should have done this years ago.'"

To prepare for the process of getting certified, Powell and Cummings needed to devise a systematic approach to making green improvements. They did, and methodically went about the task of modifying their water systems and energy requirements, tweaking their waste management program and bolstering their already-strong social involvements within the community, among numerous other tasks.

KEEPING CLEAN
Staff members at every Sandals and Beaches resort are involved in local beach cleanups as part of the company's environmental program.

The process and systems that need to be certified by **Green Globe 21** require a hotel's **serious commitment.**

Every Amenity

When guests arrive at Sandals and Beaches resorts, they are greeted with warm smiles, cold champagne and a colorful amenity kit. The tote, emblazoned with a Sandals or Beaches logo, contains an assortment of must-have toiletry items for guests on a Caribbean vacation: shampoo, conditioner, body lotion, and aloe vera gel.

Associated Manufacturers Limited, a Jamaican company that specializes in developing customized room amenities for the hospitality industry, has manufactured the kits for Sandals since 1991.

While it may have been simpler to contract this business overseas, where it had been traditionally produced, Butch Stewart is committed to efficient local production and recognized Associated Manufacturer's entrepreneurial efforts, say company officials. Stewart endorsed the company and is pleased it has met the challenge of keeping up with production and high-quality standards in accordance with Sandals' unprecedented growth.

Today, with more than eighty employees, Associated Manufacturers develops products for local and overseas markets. They include Jamaica Joe suntan products, Icelike perfumes and colognes, and the popular Busha Browne and Scotts brand of sauces, seasoning, jams, and condiments. In 2000, the company was recognized for its accomplishments when the Jamaica Exporters Association named it "Champion Exporter."

As it looks to the future, Associated Manufacturers is fully committed to the development of new products for the expanding global marketplace.

Bottom photos: Sandals Resorts International

On November 18, 1998, Sandals Negril was Green Globe 21 certified. It was the fifth resort in the world to be designated as such and the very first all-inclusive resort. Butch Stewart was presented with the certification documents for Sandals Negril at the World Travel Market in London, where he declared that all of his resorts would be Green Globe certified within three years.

Now the successful pet project of Powell and Cummings was to be rolled out to all other Sandals properties. Richard May, an integral member of the Sandals Negril team that oversaw the initial environmental preparations, was put in charge of setting up a detailed program that included green teams at all the resorts, which would promote environmental responsibility.

"When you decide to implement an environmental management system, the first thing you have to do is literally change the culture," says May, group manager of environmental affairs for Sandals Resorts International. "We developed a thorough training manual and started to make staff aware of the new initiative. Then we went to work hiring and training environmental managers for each resort."

Today, Sandals environmental managers oversee the integrity of the program, which supports environmental practices that reduce energy and water consumption, improve solid waste and wastewater disposal,

Cool Runnings Spring Water

Drink It Up!

In 1997, Horace Peterkin, general manager of Sandals Montego Bay, was searching for "liquid sunshine." He found it at a protected natural spring nestled in the misty mountains of Montpelier, fifteen hundred feet above Montego Bay. "I immediately developed the area and erected a water plant," recalls Peterkin. "Our mission is to bottle Jamaica's most authentic spring water," says Peterkin. "We call it 'Cool Runnings,' a Jamaican expression meaning 'no problem, life is good, take care on your journey.'"

Cool Runnings became an instant hit. The beverage is the official bottled water of the Reggae Boyz, Jamaica's national soccer team, the Air Jamaica Jazz & Blues Festival, and Reggae Sumfest.

"Most rewarding are our charitable concerns, particularly our sponsorship of the annual under-seventeen soccer competition in my home village of Somerton," says Peterkin.

"We want to be for the Jamaica beverage industry what Bob Marley is for reggae music."

HORACE PETERKIN
OWNER

prevent air pollution, protect marine life, and foster strong bonds with local communities.

"We are involved locally with beach cleanups and support programs in conjunction with marine societies like Friends of the Sea and the Negril Coral Reef Preservation Society," says May. "Now that the program is up and running, part of our focus includes research and development. For example, we're looking at the possibility of putting up a windmill on one of our properties in Ocho Rios to provide the resorts in that area with their own electricity backed by solar power and batteries."

Now, with all of their resorts Green Globe certified, Sandals can claim the honor of being the first all-inclusive chain in the Caribbean to have accomplished this venerable achievement.

"To me this is priceless," says May. "If we can get people to understand that, at the end of the day, your child or my child can come and enjoy the beach in the same or better condition than we enjoyed it as children, then that is an accomplishment worth working for."

In addition to being good corporate citizens themselves, for the past several years Sandals has enacted a rather innovative program in order to help raise social consciousness. And it has done it through the media.

SEEING GREEN

Sandals senior staffers accept the Green Globe 21 award. Pictured left to right are Michael Darby, general manager; Richard May, group director, environmental affairs; Carl Hendriks, general manager; and Kashmie Ali, regional director, Eastern Caribbean.

On November 18, 1998,
Sandals Negril was
Green Globe 21 certified.

CONSCIENTIOUS CORRESPONDENTS

In 1994, Sandals established the Sandals Regional Eco-Journalism Awards in association with the University of the West Indies' Caribbean Institute of Mass Communication. The competition offers cash awards for outstanding articles or programs on environmental issues that appear in the Caribbean mass media. Journalists are encouraged to submit entries addressing areas that have an impact on the Caribbean environment, are analytical and show depth of research, and are fair and balanced.

Why does Sandals go to these lengths? "Because part of our business is the business of the environment," states Patrick Lynch, director of finance and planning for Sandals Resorts International. "Without a good and clean environment, you can't have a decent hotel operation, either socially, culturally or physically. The program arose because at the time a lot of Caribbean coverage on the environment was very poor. We wanted to educate and push journalists to cover the environment more. We know that the press is often the catalyst that influences people to push governments to make sure environmental issues are addressed."

Submissions poured in on subjects ranging from beach erosion to energy management to air pollution. And winning entries actually encouraged governments to help with various environmental measures.

Sandals has continued to sponsor this auspicious project in an ongoing effort to build public awareness of environmental matters. As with Sandals' many other initiatives, the program continues to evolve, getting better and better.

"One of the things we learned is that journalists wanted more training," Patrick Lynch continues. "We listened to their needs and added a seminar component into the program in 2001. It turned into a major two-day conference whereby Sandals invited experts in eco-journalism from the U.K., Canada and the Caribbean to have an open exchange with Caribbean journalists."

Indeed, the seminar, held at Beaches Grande Sport, included noted speakers. Among the many were Frances Cairncross of *The Economist* speaking on globalization, economics and trade; Dr. Kathryn Monk of Iwokrama speaking on the many programs at the Iwokrama International Centre for Rainforest Conservation and Development; Wahad Ally of the Barbados Nation Publishing Company speaking on media and the environment; and Hamish McRae of *The Independent* discussing the future and environmental issues.

Ever passionate about the cause, Sandals continues to be environmentally active, dedicating the necessary time and resources to champion worthwhile programs.

ECO ESSAYIST
Matthew Falloon of Guyana's *Stabroek News*, left, accepts an award for his environmental entry from Sandals General Manager Michael Darby.

Shell Jamaica

Energy Solutions

Shell is regarded in the energy business for its leadership, innovation, customer service, and fulfillment. In addition, Shell provides a wide range of energy solutions to its customers across the globe.

"Shell's partnership with Sandals has been mutually rewarding," says Mario Vulinovich, country chairman of Shell Jamaica. "Of the many achievements and awards Sandals and Beaches have received, we are especially pleased with Sandals' Green Globe Certification. This recognition is consistent with Shell's focus on sustainable development, particularly protecting our environment and managing our resources in order to respect the needs of future generations. Like Sandals, we are committed to making a positive impact on our society both now and in the future."

"We are especially pleased with Sandals' Green Globe Certification."

MARIO VULINOVICH
COUNTRY CHAIRMAN

Delivering Dream

Both Air Canada Vacations and Sandals share a mutual passion for the pursuit of perfection and top-notch service.

Air Canada Vacations, one of the top ten tourism companies in Canada, specializes in the distribution of best-value sun and cruise leisure vacation packages. The company has enjoyed a long-standing relationship with Sandals.

"It began long ago when all-inclusive vacations were not in vogue," recalls Jim Proctor, Air Canada Vacations vice-president of product development, who at the time was contracting Jamaica for Air Canada Vacations.

"The Sandals concept, however, was innovative and caused a buzz in the industry. The team at Sandals proposed an all-inclusive concept for couples only. By doing that, they went against the conventional wisdom of catering to singles and families with children.

Top left photo: Sandals Resorts International

Vacations

But Butch Stewart knew the market he was going after and he took a big chance," explains Proctor.

"There's always been something special about Sandals ever since its emergence onto the travel scene. We anticipated that Butch had plans to be a major Caribbean hotelier and we wanted to do business with him. After a couple of knocks on the door, our twenty-year relationship began."

The two men met in Montego Bay, Jamaica, and had an instant camaraderie. "I was struck by Butch's larger-than-life persona," recalls Proctor. "Over the years, I've come to know Butch as a very dynamic guy with big vision. He's self-made and ambitious to the extreme. Obstacles don't deter him. He charges on no matter what. And, Butch is definitely not someone who takes no for an answer!"

At a time when the vast majority of properties in the Caribbean, and specifically on Jamaica, were running as European Plan hotels,

Air Canada Vacations took a risk when it added Sandals Montego Bay to its product line. Before long, the gamble paid off in huge dividends.

"People very quickly grasped the concept and it skyrocketed. Today, the whole industry has changed to an all-inclusive market and Sandals is still considered the leader, which I believe is due to attention to quality and excellence, which has always been at the top of Sandals' list of priorities. The hotel group is renowned for keeping its properties constantly upgraded."

Twenty years since its initial meeting with Sandals, Air Canada Vacations has become the number one supplier in Canada of Sandals and Beaches resorts. The honors and accolades for its stellar achievements keep piling in. To date, Air Canada Vacations has received several prestigious Ultra Awards from Sandals Resorts, including "Canada's Top Producing Tour Operator" for six consecutive years.

"The Air Canada Vacations client profile is an ideal match for Sandals and Beaches," says Proctor. "It has to do with the level of quality and choices we provide, including spacious airline seats, free advance seat selection, executive-class seating on Air Canada and Aeroplan, and our frequent-flyer program."

Most of all, both Air Canada Vacations and Sandals share a mutual passion for the pursuit of perfection and top-notch service, he adds.

"We are like-minded travel companies and that is what has made our relationship strong over the past two decades," says Proctor. "When Sandals came in and changed the industry, Air Canada Vacations jumped on board and supported its vision. Butch Stewart and the Sandals team were true motivators in changing and leading this industry. It's been a remarkable experience to work with Sandals and to watch both our companies grow."

The rest, as they say, is history.

Photo: Tropical Imaging

11 Liquid Assets

FLYING ABOVE THE TURKS AND
CAICOS ISLANDS IS QUITE A SIGHT.
SURROUNDING WATERS BOAST
THE THIRD-LARGEST CORAL REEF
SYSTEM IN THE WORLD.

Every November, more than forty thousand movers and shakers in the travel industry descend on London for the World Travel Market, the preeminent global tourism and travel exposition. Walk the aisles and find tourist boards from Mallorca to Mozambique, hoteliers from St. Kitts to Sweden, and transport companies from Zurich to Zambia promoting themselves. Here, destinations are launched and deals are cut. And, should you be seeking a resort group to purchase your new property, the World Travel Market is *the* place to shop.

Sandals promised to deliver a top-class luxury resort within eighteen months.

A PROPERTY ON PROVO

During the November 1995 World Travel Market, government officials from the Turks and Caicos Islands approached executives at Sandals and made their pitch: The newly constructed two-hundred-room Royal Bay Resort and Villas, on the island of Providenciales, was for sale. Would Sandals be interested?

A few weeks later, Stewart and his team were headed thirty miles southeast of the Bahamas to Providenciales, or Provo, one of some forty cays that comprise the Turks and Caicos Islands. Flying above the archipelago is quite a sight: Surrounding waters boast the third-largest coral reef system in the world within 193 square miles of amazingly crystal-clear water. The Sandals team landed on Provo and was whisked off to Grace Bay to view the Royal Bay Resort and Villas. The property has an interesting background. In 1986, the Turks and Caicos government leased the site to Canadian developers who had agreed to construct the property for a large hotel chain. Construction was seriously delayed and, by 1991, there was only a concrete remnant on the prime beachfront spot. This unfinished blot on the landscape spurred the government into demanding a performance bond, thereby insuring completion of the project should developers default. When the property was still unfinished by 1993, the government obliged Canadian-based Zurich Insurance to respond and complete the project. Finally, in October 1995, the property was opened with the understanding that it would be sold.

A SHORE THING
Above: The vision of Sandals' new resort on the Turks and Caicos Islands turned quickly into reality. Right: The powder sand beaches of Provo go on for miles.

The Sandals team liked what it saw, on property and off—an exotic, unspoiled locale with pristine beaches, one of the world's best dive sites, friendly people, a stable government, and a brand-new resort on a choice twelve-mile stretch of beach along Grace Bay. Sandals purchased the Royal Bay Resort and Villas in January 1996, within a month of the initial visit. In return, Sandals promised to deliver a top-class luxury resort within eighteen months.

Now owned by Sandals, the resort continued to be run as a European Plan hotel under the Royal Bay name. However, Sandals, the master of all-inclusive resorts, soon realized that in order for the resort to be successful, it would have to be converted from a European Plan to an all-inclusive.

"Although the physical property was new, it needed to be 'Sandalized,'" muses John Lynch, executive vice president of sales worldwide for Unique Vacations. "Given the success we were having with Beaches Negril, a decision was made to remodel the Royal Bay into a Beaches resort."

Pricewaterhouse Coopers

Professionals to Count On

As the Sandals team branched out to the Eastern Caribbean, it sought companies to do business with that shared its core values: excellence, teamwork and leadership. PricewaterhouseCoopers Eastern Caribbean, dedicated to the same ideals, has long been an integral part of the region.

Antigua Managing Partner Charles Walwyn has worked with Sandals for more than twelve years, ever since the hotel group opened Sandals Antigua in 1991. "It's certainly been a pleasure to work with the Sandals group and to watch them continue to expand in the Eastern Caribbean," says Walwyn. Indeed, as Sandals has expanded within the region, the team from PricewaterhouseCoopers working with it has grown too.

St. Lucia Managing Partner Anthony Atkinson has been an integral part of the Sandals expansion in the Eastern Caribbean, providing professional services to the three Sandals properties located on St. Lucia of the four in the Eastern Caribbean. "We, of course, look forward to our continued long-term relationship with Sandals," says Atkinson.

An Entertaining Experience

Margaritaville Caribbean is the brainchild of Jamaican entrepreneurs and best friends Brian Jardim and Ian Dear. In 1994, with years of experience between them, the duo decided the time was right to introduce Montego Bay to a fun and exciting place that the whole family could enjoy and where both locals and visitors could relax and have a good time. They dreamed of a cool place on the waterfront where good food and drink flow and the fun never stops—in a word, Margaritaville!

And so the first Margaritaville was born. Featuring Jamaica's first waterslide, a mouthwatering all-day menu, and nightlife that really swings, their first venture was a runaway success.

Next, the fun-loving friends opened Margaritaville's alter ego, Marguerite's Seafood by the Sea, right next door. This elegant, intimate water's-edge seafood restaurant is now acknowledged as one of the island's finest.

Less than a year later, Jardim and Dear unveiled the second restaurant in the chain, Margueritaville Negril. On the sands of world-famous seven-mile beach, the 'Ville Negril has a casual, bohemian vibe in sync with the laid-back resort town.

In 2000, Jardim and Dear began negotiations with singer Jimmy Buffett to become the Caribbean franchise holders for Jimmy Buffett's Margaritaville, and by 2001, the deal was sealed. The existing restaurants were re-branded as Margaritavilles and a new restaurant, Air Margaritaville, debuted at Sangster International Airport in Montego Bay.

The largest Jamaican Margaritaville, Margaritaville Ocho Rios, debuted in February 2002. On the beach at the Island Village entertainment and shopping complex, it quickly became a hit, especially with local partygoers and cruise ship passengers.

Jardim and Dear are always on the lookout for ways to refine and expand the concept, and they plan to open more locations throughout the Caribbean. As Jamaicans say, "soon come."

Fixtures and Fittings

As the largest distributor of waterworks and plumbing products in the United States, Ferguson Enterprises understands the behind-the-scenes business of building properties such as Sandals and Beaches resorts. "We are proud of our fifteen-year partnership with Sandals," says Bob Cerrone, Ferguson's general manager. "Through the years, we've worked closely with the hotel group's design team on product selection in order to furnish some twenty-five properties with the latest and greatest products."

From the renovation of existing properties to the development of new ones, Ferguson always stands ready and willing to go the extra mile for Sandals to keep its idyllic properties at their peak performance and at the forefront of the resort industry.

With more than seven hundred locations in forty-nine states, and in Puerto Rico, Mexico, Barbados, and Trinidad, Ferguson stocks a huge

inventory of parts and supplies, and consistently goes out of its way to quickly locate and deliver hard-to-find specialty items.

Ferguson was built on the successful development of plumbing distribution capabilities unparalleled in the industry today.

For that reason, Ferguson has built an impeccable reputation among all of its customers, including Sandals. "We are truly proud of our reputation, but you'll never see Ferguson rest on its laurels," says Cerrone, "unless of course, we're lucky enough to find ourselves vacationing at a beautiful Sandals or Beaches resort!"

A $20 million transformation commenced. Rooms were fitted with Sandals' signature four-poster mahogany beds; grounds were upgraded with lush tropical foliage, which was no small feat due to the dry climate. In keeping with the tradition of offering guests a multitude of dining choices, new gourmet specialty restaurants were added. Other additions included a Kids Kamp, a SEGA games center and a full-service European spa. Since diving is understandably one of the most popular water sports in the Turks and Caicos islands, a first-class dive operation was up and running in no time. The "new" property was named Beaches Turks & Caicos Resort & Spa.

Travel Agent Magazine

Keeping Agents in the Know

When it comes to keeping the travel agent community informed, Travel Agent magazine is the only national newsweekly in the United States geared best to serve the travel industry. Travel Agent magazine is designed to interpret and analyze news, trends and issues to enable owners, managers and frontline travel agents to thrive and profit in an ever-changing marketplace. Travel Agent is read by qualified, influential decision makers in the industry and reaches every ARC-, IATAN- and CLIA-certified travel agency.

For travel agents worldwide seeking access to breaking news in the industry, Travel Agent offers TravelAgentCentral.com. Here, travel agents can log on to Travel Agent University, an Internet classroom for travel agents that allows them to earn ICTA credits; to the Official Travel Industry Directory, a comprehensive travel industry resource; to Premier Resorts and Hotels, a booking engine for luxury vacations; and to Luxury Travel Expo Web site, the largest gathering of travel agents worldwide who specialize in luxury travel.

dive in

Among the many water-sports amenities that the Sandals chain offers its guests, a favorite is the scuba diving program. What began with one small dive boat at Sandals Montego Bay has today grown into the largest dive program in the Caribbean. More than thirty thousand guests, both beginners and experienced certified divers, take part in the resort course each year so they can qualify to dive with Sandals' trained professional staff.

Remarks Noylis Amair, group director of water sports for Sandals Resorts International: "All of our team members are extremely proud of the professional dive program that we've built over the years. We're committed to providing the finest dive operation in the Caribbean, with the goal of getting our guests excited about the program and turning them on to this terrific adventure sport."

Sandals is also dedicated to protecting the living seas. "We have a mandate to be environmentally responsible and recognize that the sea is a precious place," says Amair. "Sandals supports local marine parks and ensures that environmental sensitivity comes first." To that end, all guests who choose to dive are briefed on the importance of protecting the seas and are advised not to remove anything or damage the coral reefs with their fins. Several resorts also partner with PADI (Professional Association of Diving Instructors) for ongoing beach cleanups.

Today, the Turks and Caicos Islands is regarded as a hot spot among the jet set … and the family set, too.

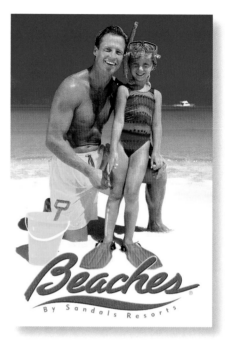

lure

So enticed was a young thirteen-year-old boy by the colorful Beaches brochure he was reading that, in the summer of 1997 before today's tightened airline security, the youngster fled the downtown Miami shelter where he was living in search of the resort paradise. With no money or passport, the gutsy kid somehow slipped onto an airplane headed for Montego Bay, Jamaica. He managed to get through Customs before Sandals airport manager, Don Smith, questioned him and then arranged for his return to Miami.

When Butch Stewart heard about the incident, he was impressed by the lad's resourcefulness. Stewart quickly crafted a way that could eventually get the boy to Beaches and at the same time serve to inspire the child. He extended an offer to the boy: "Maintain a C average in school and Beaches will fly you and your family to the Jamaican resort next summer."

BACK TO BEACHES

Beaches Turks & Caicos Resort & Spa opened in April 1997. The resort was dazzling and proved yet again that Butch Stewart and the Sandals group had the Midas touch. Says former Minister of Tourism for Jamaica Anthony Abrahams: "What Butch does so well is to fix up what we call in the industry 'old concrete.' He takes over an existing property, pulls it apart, reconfigures it, hires excellent staff, trains them well, applies a formula and there you have it, another award-winning Sandals resort."

With the addition of Beaches Turks & Caicos Resort & Spa, the island received an unprecedented level of exposure. "Beaches truly transformed the Turks and Caicos Islands as a destination," remarks John Lynch.

Indeed, backed by Sandals' marketing machine, the Turks and Caicos Islands became a major player in Caribbean tourism. More than $2.5 million was spent advertising and promoting the new resort—big-time exposure for a Caribbean destination with a modest tourism budget. With the Turks and Caicos name now plastered on billboards and buses, on display in travel agency windows, and in print advertising and on television, the destination gained market clout. Today, the Turks and Caicos Islands is regarded as a hot spot among the jet set … and the family set, too. In fact, Beaches Turks & Caicos went on to become so popular that, in 1998, seventy-two rooms were added. The following year, the resort expanded again, with the addition of 166 rooms, built around a quaint French Village, and Pirate's Island, a water-themed entertainment area and haven for kids.

PIRATES OF THE CARIBBEAN

Pirate's Island, pictured at right, is a water-themed entertainment center designed with kids in mind.

"Mr. Stewart wanted to create a
special place
on the property just for kids."

Recalls one former interior designer for Sandals, "Mr. Stewart wanted to create a special place on the property just for kids. His vision was to incorporate a 1950s-style diner, a Microsoft® XBOX Game Oasis

Video Game Center, and a large pool with waterslides, but we were unsure how to tie all of it together. One Friday, he called me into the office and said, 'See what you can come up with.' I thought that pirates would be a good theme since we were a Caribbean company, and I sketched some plans that weekend to include a pirate ship as the focal point. On Monday, I presented the sketches to Mr. Stewart and he said, 'Wow!' He called the architect Graham Sant on the phone and said, 'Make it happen.'"

Expedia.com

Sea and Surf

When Expedia, the leading provider of online travel services for leisure and business travelers, started its vacation package business in January 2001, Sandals and Beaches resorts were the first Caribbean hotels to be featured.

"Butch Stewart and his team recognized that the Internet would alter the way consumers bought travel," says Gene Harden, a director for Expedia. "They immediately embraced Expedia, and we started selling Sandals resort packages through our new booking channel."

Today, Expedia, headquartered in Bellevue, Washington, is the number one online travel site, with more than eighteen million users who visit Expedia for great deals in travel every month.

Managing Well

When Sandals Dunn's River Golf Resort & Spa in Ocho Rios, Jamaica, was being constructed, the owners hired Jamaican-based Implementation Ltd. to act as its professional project manager. Under the guidance of Founding Director Jeremy Brown, the team at Implementation Ltd. helped carry the idea of Sandals from concept to completion. Backed by Implementation's expertise in feasibility studies, project accounting, design coordination, and construction management, Sandals was able to open a winner of a resort on Jamaica's north coast.

"Ever since our initial meeting with Butch Stewart in 1989, we have worked closely with him and the Sandals team," says Keith Rigbye, project manager for Implementation Ltd. "We highly regard our relationship with Sandals and enjoy the opportunity to work with an organization that shows such drive, vigor and enthusiasm."

Drive and vigor indeed! Since 1989, Implementation Ltd. has worked with Sandals on numerous projects, including Sandals Royal Bahamian Resort & Spa, Beaches Turks and Caicos Resort & Spa and the soon-to-debut Sandals Whitehouse European Village & Spa on Jamaica.

In addition to its reputation as the Caribbean's premier project management company in tourism development, Implementation Ltd. is also regarded for its successful projects in the residential, commercial, corporate, industrial and medical sectors.

Certainly, as a Caribbean-based company, Implementation knows the lay of the land. "We truly understand the region and its idiosyncrasies, both environmental and cultural," says Brown. "Our clients benefit from an internationally diverse team with a combined sixty-six years of hands-on experience in the region."

Top photo: Sandals Resorts International

> *"These hotels and resorts represent luxury at its best, and our robes are part of their product line."*
>
> DANNY TUATY
> PRESIDENT

Cozy

Ty, Ty, & Ty found its niche in the hotel and resort industry.

For more than thirty years, Ty, Ty, & Ty, a third-generation bathrobe and towel manufacturing company, has been servicing luxury resorts and hotels with its assortment of oh-so-soft textiles. The family business began as a small bathrobe mill in South America. Danny Tuaty, president of Ty, Ty, & Ty, recalls his frequent visits to the mill as a young child, where he watched the terry looms run. "Observing the manufacturing process was a great learning experience for me. I found out from a very young age that hard work and dedication are necessary ingredients in order to

Coverup

have had to live up to hotel guests' discerning tastes. Certainly our customers depend on us to provide the finest quality robes and towels at competitive prices."

Ty, Ty, & Ty began working with the Sandals team in 2000, when the resort group approached the company with the idea of manufacturing an exclusively designed bathrobe. The custom robes would be placed in all Sandals and Beaches suites. "The concept was to create an inviting tropical robe that would make a guest want to lounge by the pool while sipping a cool drink," recalls William Serbin, executive vice president of Ty, Ty, & Ty. The result was a tropical-weight kimono bathrobe, which fit with the Sandals ambience. "It's amazing how many calls we receive from Sandals guests telling us how much they enjoyed our robes," adds Serbin.

Today, Ty, Ty, & Ty operates three fully vertical mills in South America, Turkey and Egypt. The product line has grown to include not only bathrobes but also fine towels and sheets. "We have always prided ourselves on delivering the highest quality robes and towels, says Tuaty. "For more than ten years, we have maintained an unmatched level of service, quick delivery and attention to detail.

become successful in the manufacturing business." After earning his degree in textile engineering from Philadelphia College of Textiles and Science, Tuaty moved his company and family to Miami, Florida.

Once in Miami, Ty, Ty, & Ty started to take off. The company found its niche in the hotel and resort industry; and today, it is regarded as one of the leading suppliers of terry and sheeting products. Many of the company's clients are among the top four- and five-star properties throughout the United States and the Caribbean. "These hotels and resorts represent luxury at its best and our robes are part of their product line," says Tuaty. "We, too,

Brian Roper, group director of operations for Sandals Resorts International, far left, and several Sandals general managers gather at an industry event.

EACH ONE, TEACH ONE

Along with a sparkling new resort or two, one of the most significant benefits that Caribbean countries receive from having Sandals grace their shores is the organization's commitment to employing and training locals.

According to Turks and Caicos Tourism Minister Oswald Skippings: "Sandals lived up to its commitment to Turks and Caicos by not only providing a quality resort in record time, but by being good corporate citizens. They employed and trained 234 Turks islanders at their new resort."

Training is one of the key ingredients to Sandals' success, and the chain is noted in the industry as having one of the most comprehensive programs. All facets of training are underscored with the resort chain's philosophy, "each one, teach one"—a hands-on, integrated approach that started in the very early days of the company and continues to this day.

Sandals Resorts International Managing Director Merrick Fray explains: "Anytime we go into a new Caribbean destination, an integral component is cross-training. We always send some of our Jamaican staff to work hand in hand with staff at the new property and, in return, new staff is sent to our resorts in Jamaica. It provides a way for us to integrate the people and the culture of our organization."

Just as important as investing in concrete, Sandals invests in people.

Just as important as investing in concrete, Sandals invests in people. "We provide customer-service training to kitchen staff, to housecleaning, and even to our ground maintenance staff," notes Dr. Ben Henry, group director of training for Sandals Resorts International. "At the very core is our attitude that everyone contributes to the tourism product."

In an industry noted for turnover, Sandals is the exception. Peruse a list of staff in any facet of the organization and you will find longtime team members with tenures of seventeen, eighteen, and twenty-plus years of service. You will also find resident managers who started as busboys, and general managers who began their careers as Playmakers. "We have a philosophy of promoting from within," says Brian Roper, Sandals group director of operations, who himself started as food and beverage manager in 1981 and rose up through the ranks. "Senior managers keep a focused eye on staff," he explains. "When we see rising stars, we will stretch them, challenge them and always provide them with the tools and training needed to ascend within the organization."

Sant Associates
Architect

Well-Designed

Sant Associates are builders of dreams. As architects for Sandals, the four-person firm, led by Graham Sant, has designed the latest and greatest Sandals and Beaches resorts.

Sant and Associates began their association with Sandals as architects for the Royal Bay hotel on the Turks and Caicos Islands, which Sandals acquired in 1996. "Mr. Stewart hired our firm to design the second phase of Beaches Turks and Caicos Resort & Spa," says Graham Sant. "From there, we went on to design the second phase of Sandals Royal Bahamian Resort & Spa and have continued handling nearly all of Sandals and Beaches architectural projects."

With the French Village at Beaches Turks and Caicos Resort & Spa, Sunset Bluff at Sandals Regency St. Lucia and the soon-to-open Sandals Whitehouse European Village & Spa on Jamaica under its belt, Sant Associates is beautifying the Caribbean, one resort at a time.

"We're always trying to give Sandals guests a new experience."

GRAHAM SANT
PRESIDENT

"I am convinced that the most important component in any business is the human element."

— Butch Stewart

In 1995, the company established the Sandals Training and Development Institute, which Chairman Butch Stewart calls "Sandals University."

Dr. Ben Henry, elaborating on the education staff members receive, says, "Many of our staff cannot travel abroad for studies. So we brought college to them. We established a relationship with Hocking College, in Ohio, whereby we fly professors down to conduct our in-house associate degree program. For two years, staff members attend classes here at Sandals and then, at the end of the two years, they go to Ohio and attend one semester in order to receive an associate in arts degree. I'm very proud to say that nearly two hundred team members have received associate degrees through that program."

With such a serious commitment to top-notch tourism training, it's evident why many Caribbean countries welcome Sandals to their shores.

TEAM LEADER
Butch Stewart, at right, surrounded by Sandals general managers. He considers his management team the best in the business.

Renwick & Company Ltd.

Top Shoppers

Christopher Renwick knows how to make things grow. . .especially when it comes to business. In 1966, the young entrepreneur from St. Lucia started a small company importing and distributing agricultural chemicals. "We saw an opportunity just as bananas were emerging as big business," says Renwick.

Sales went well, especially due to Renwick's passionate dedication to the customer. "I'm a fiend for service," says Renwick. In no time, the company diversified into Honda motorcycles, Australian wines, building materials, and electrical appliances.

Today, Renwick & Company "shops the world" for its clients, which include Sandals Resorts, and they distribute everything from vegetable seeds, to consumer care products, to pharmaceuticals. With a dynamic team and commitment to the community, the company is poised to continue growing stronger than ever.

"I've always said the customer must come first."

CHRISTOPHER RENWICK
MANAGING DIRECTOR

12 Love Is All You Need

THE SATISFACTION I GET COMES FROM
THE POWERFUL ORGANIZATION WE'VE
BUILT AND THE CONTRIBUTION THAT
WE'VE MADE TO THE CARIBBEAN AND
THE TRAVEL INDUSTRY.

Gordon "Butch" Stewart

Enter the Projects Office at Sandals Resorts International in Montego Bay on any given day and the place is bustling. The same holds true for the various other nerve centers that manage design projects among hundreds of other important assignments. These workplaces are filled with architectural drawings, blueprints, bolts of fabric, samples of tiles, chairs, light fixtures, and all other matters related to the planning, refurbishing and construction of Sandals' multimillion-dollar resorts.

LINE OF EXISTIN
SLAB.

6'-0"

"Mr. Stewart still manages to keep his finger on everything."

Why are the department offices of Sandals' Projects always so busy? The answer is best summed up by Jaime Stewart, Butch Stewart's daughter: "When you have a product that works and makes money, you have to continuously inject that money back into your product, not just to maintain it but to make what you have even better. Growing up it was made clear to me that you build a good name through genuine quality, not through quantity. The first business mantra I learned from dad is 'you've got to spend money to make money.' I never appreciated what that meant until my days working in the Projects department. We worked day and night on construction sites clearing containers filled with fabulous new furniture, carpets and fixtures, spot-checking each and every one, and making sure they were flawlessly installed. The team members of the Projects department are some of the company's silent superheros. They help to make the hotels as beautiful and fantastic as they are."

To this day, Butch Stewart, the original Trader King, is still a stickler for keeping his hotels meticulous. And, his passion for setting trends and staying one step ahead of everybody in the industry persists. Eighteen-hour days are still the norm. Standards are set ever higher. Says Stewart: "I am generally very easygoing and friendly, but I am not easygoing when it comes to standards. I will shout and scream to get the job done properly."

Eleanor Miller, Sandals group director of projects, adds, "Mr. Stewart has moved the bar so many times. Those of us who have worked with him for years have grown accustomed to reaching that bar, which he continues to set higher and higher."

Everyone working for Sandals knows Stewart is involved and instrumental in all aspects of the business. "He still manages to keep his finger on everything," says Stewart's longtime assistant, Betty Jo Desnoes. "I don't know how he manages to do it, yet he does, down to the minute details. I believe it's based on his method of communication and work ethic. He talks to everyone, from gardeners tending to the lawns on property to prime ministers. And, he uses every minute of the day. A weekend is not shutdown; he's never out of touch."

VIP VISIT
Butch Stewart takes St. Lucia Prime Minister Dr. Kenny Anthony and other government dignitaries on a tour of Sandals Grande St. Lucian Spa & Beach Resort under construction.

Part of the Sandals success story is credited to the company's ability to continually meet the vacation demands of its clients. For example, by 1999, families, singles, couples, and business incentive groups were filling to capacity the two Beaches resorts—Beaches Negril Resort & Spa and Beaches Turks & Caicos Resort & Spa. The time had come to expand. From 1999 through 2002, the company opened two new resorts, which are today marketed under the Beaches name. They are Beaches Sandy Bay in Negril and Beaches Boscobel Resort & Golf Club in Ocho Rios, both catering to kids, families, couples and singles.

HEAVENLY HOLIDAY
Beaches Boscobel Resort & Golf Club, pictured at right, has a host of amenities for families. A specially designed Appleton Rum bar, above, however, is just one of the hot spots on property geared to adults only.

In recent years, Beaches cornered another growing market—single parents. "This is a program that we've spearheaded in the industry," says Maggie Rivera, Unique Vacations director of public relations and sales promotions, who helped develop the program. "We created a dedicated year-round program for single parents and conducted months of research to find out what appeals to this niche market."

Beaches offers innovative on-property programs, such as a weekly reception for single parents, as well as socials and activities designed especially for single parents and their children. "There's no hotel out there that has an ongoing program like this one," Rivera points out. "Beaches is becoming symbolic with all types of families, and we're knocking directly on their door and saying, 'Hey, you, too, are a Beaches customer.'"

Beaches Boscobel Resort & Golf Club

caters to kids, families, couples and singles.

NEW AND IMPROVED

The notion of giving guests more than they expect is also reflected in the incredible recent transformation of Sandals Ocho Rios. "We wanted to create an expansive paradise that gives vacationers a variety of choices in terms of accommodations, dining and activities," says Brian Roper, group director of operations for Sandals Resorts International, about the new Sandals Grande Ocho Rios Beach & Villa Resort. The impressive 110-acre property is replete with 529 rooms and suites, 88 private and semi-private pools set in and around the lush mountains of St. Ann, seven main pools, personalized "Butler Service," twelve gourmet restaurants, 24-hour room service and in-suite dining, two full-service European spas, championship golf at Sandals Golf & Country Club and a top-notch water-sports complex.

GARDEN VARIETY
One of 244 villa suites at Sandals Grande Ocho Rios Beach & Villa Resort, pictured at left. The resort, below, is set into a lush mountainside.

MLT Vacations Inc.

Travel Benefits

MLT Vacations Inc.®, the tour operator of Northwest Airlines WorldVacations® and Worry-Free Vacations®, and a wholly owned subsidiary of Northwest Airlines®, has been a proud partner of Sandals for over twenty years.

"We sincerely value our long-standing and successful partnership with Sandals," says MLT Vacations President and CEO Beth Shultis. "And we look forward to many more years of working together to deliver innovative, exciting vacations for our mutual customers."

MLT Vacations is one of the top producers for Sandals Resorts. In 2002, for the third year in a row, MLT Vacations earned the third-place award for "Top Producing Tour Operator in the United States" at the Ultra Awards, an award ceremony acknowledging Sandals' top travel partners. Other awards over the years have included the "Top Suite Seller" in 2001 for Sandals Dunn's River and in 2002 for Sandals Montego Bay.

"We sincerely value our long-standing partnership with Sandals."

BETH SHULTIS
PRESIDENT AND CEO

Set amid Jamaica's lush northern coast, Royal Plantation Ocho Rios, Jamaica is the island's first-ever member of the Leading Small Hotels of the World. Below: Butch Stewart and daughter, Jaime, applaud as the red ribbon is cut at the opening ceremony.

RESORTS FOR THE NEW MILLENNIUM

When the new century was ushered in, the Sandals team rang it in with—you guessed it—another new resort property.

However, Royal Plantation Ocho Rios, Jamaica would be developed and marketed as its own boutique brand. "Royal Plantation was a restoration project like no other," says Jaime Stewart, managing director for Royal Plantation Ocho Rios, Jamaica. "When the property originally opened in 1957 as Plantation Inn, it was *the* hotel on Jamaica. Kings and queens, politicians and movie stars flocked to the charming hotel, which personified Jamaican glamour and elegance. My passion lies in merging Royal Plantation's old-time nostalgia with the modern luxuries found in today's premier hotels around the world."

Indeed, Jaime Stewart and her team has worked tirelessly to upgrade the seventy-seven-suite luxury property, which offers its guests a choice of either a traditional European Plan (EP) or an all-inclusive Royal Plan, award-winning dining options, butler service, daily English tea service and many other exclusive amenities. No expense was spared: Guest rooms were outfitted with Mascioni Italian bedding and 100 percent down duvets, and also pillow menus. Dining options cater to refined sensibilities. "We partnered with Veuve Clicqot to develop C I BAR, the Caribbean's first and only champagne and caviar bar," Jaime Stewart points out.

Accolades and awards for the Green Globe–certified property include a AAA Four Diamond rating, three American Academy of Hospitality Science Five Star Diamond Awards and winner of the Resort and Great Hotels Connoisseurs Choice Award for 2004. Royal Plantation Ocho Rios, Jamaica is a member of The Leading Small Hotels of the World and Leading Spas of the World. "The recognition Royal Plantation has received is exceptional," says Jaime Stewart. "Most near and dear to my heart is our affiliation with The Leading Small Hotels of the World, which maintains scrupulously high standards for resorts in terms of the quality they expect when they conduct inspections."

Colombian Emeralds International is regarded as one of the largest duty-free jewelers in the world and the foremost emerald jeweler.

Sparkle

More than thirty years ago, when merchants from Colombian Emeralds were searching for a setting to open their first emerald and jewelry shop, they looked to the natural beauty of the islands and opened two small stores in the Spanish/South American section of the International Bazaar, one of the oldest shopping areas in Freeport, the Bahamas. Visitors flocked to the bazaar and to Colombian Emeralds.

Over the years, the business grew and thrived. Today, the company, now known as Colombian Emeralds International, has expanded to sixteen destinations and has thirty-five store locations throughout the Caribbean and the Bahamas. Colombian Emeralds International is regarded as one of the largest duty-free jewelers in the world and the foremost emerald jeweler. Its reputation for offering a vast selection of emeralds and jewelry at excellent duty-free prices has attracted clients worldwide.

Plenty

Where do the precious gems and jewelry come from? Buyers for Colombian Emeralds International travel to destinations around the globe in search of original yet timeless designs in fine emeralds, precious jewelry and prestigious watches. Emeralds are purchased loose directly from Colombia.

However, there are some regions where the company's buyers will not shop. Clients can rest assured knowing that buyers at Colombian Emeralds International fully support a policy of not purchasing diamonds that are illicitly seized and sold by rebel forces in Angola, Sierra Leone and the Democratic Republic of the Congo.

When its buyers do make a purchase, they do so directly from the source in order to be sure that clients receive the best possible quality and value. Each gemstone—emerald, diamond, sapphire, ruby, and tanzanite—is carefully selected for its color, clarity, cut, and rarity. To round out its offerings, Colombian Emeralds International also carries a selection of exclusive signature pieces.

Every jewelry purchase made at Colombian Emeralds International is accompanied by a complimentary certified appraisal, which acts as an international guarantee of authenticity. And, diamond solitaire ring purchases of a half-carat or larger come with a gratis diamond consultation or a certified appraisal from the International Gemological Institute, one of the world's most trusted sources for independent, objective documentation regarding the quality of diamonds.

A 'GRANDE' RESORT

Following Royal Plantation, the group went on to open its eleventh Sandals resort the following year. This time, Sandals returned to the island of St. Lucia, acquiring the former Hyatt Regency St. Lucia. The property is set on an exquisite part of the island along a stunning isthmus on the shores of Rodney Bay, which affords views of the bay and the mountains on one side and the distant shores of Martinique on the other.

St. Lucia's prime minister, Dr. Kenny Anthony, said at the time, "St. Lucia is very fortunate to have Sandals come to our shores once again. There can be no question that its presence has helped to place St. Lucia in the top league of Caribbean destinations. Sandals continues to be synonymous with quality, warmth, charm, excellent accommodations, and value for money."

Though the property was fairly new when Sandals took it over, Stewart spent $10 million to renovate the resort to his liking—and, more importantly, the liking of his guests. Local St. Lucian Steve Jameson, owner of Jamecob's Quality Construction Ltd., handled construction: "I've worked with Sandals since 1992, helping to build the three properties on the island. The experience has proved very special for me. I first started as a contractor, working on small construction projects for Sandals Regency St. Lucia. The company realized that I had potential, put their trust in me, and advocated for me to take on more challenging projects. A few years later, my company built a large block of suites known as the Sunset Bluff at Sandals Regency St. Lucia. When they acquired the Hyatt, I was contacted by Sandals to handle construction for the new Sandals Grande St. Lucian Spa & Beach Resort."

BUILDING BLOCKS
Sandals Grande St. Lucian Spa & Beach Resort transforms from construction site, at left and below, to its final form, pictured above. Bottom left: The resort played host to former U.S. President Clinton, pictured at right with Butch Stewart, and has a presidential suite named in Clinton's honor.

Jameson adds, "We worked night and day to renovate the property on time and construct a massive pool with what was the first-ever double-decker swim-up pool, as well as a dive pool. There was also a spa and fitness center. I was so proud to see it completed and to see how far I'd come."

During construction, government dignitaries were treated to a site tour led by a proud guide, Butch Stewart.

Commenting on the hotel group, St. Lucia's Minister of Tourism Phillip J. Pierre said at the time, "What I find extraordinary about Sandals is the level of teamwork and camaraderie that exists, which stems from the top. I've toured properties with Butch Stewart and observed him stopping to chat with everyone, from gardeners and house-keepers to managers. He considers everyone's role to be important to the hotel industry."

J.A.G. Inc.

Island Adventures

Visitors to St. Lucia stand in awe of the island's rich natural beauty, which beckons exploration. They can hike through a majestic rain forest, see picturesque waterfalls or opt for beach trips and specialized land and sea packages. Another popular attraction is Sulphur Springs, the world's only "drive-in" volcano. One way to see the island in style is to book a trip through J.A.G., St. Lucia's premier jeep safari tour company.

Owner Julian Adjodha began his operation in the year 2000 with three custom-built Land Rovers. He worked hard to grow the company and remains dedicated to his vision. Today, J.A.G. boasts a fleet of fourteen jeeps and a reputation as the leading provider of leisure jeep tours on the island.

"We're fully committed to providing the best tours on the island to ensure that our guests walk away with a memorable experience."

JULIAN ADJODHA
OWNER

" BUTCH STEWART IS AN EXTRAORDINARY CARIBBEAN PERSON. I OFTEN SAY THAT THE CARIBBEAN CAN MAKE A DIFFERENCE AND I CITE BUTCH STEWART AS AN EXAMPLE OF SOMEONE WHO DEMONSTRATES THE REAL POSSIBILITIES. WHAT IS PARTICULARLY PLEASING ABOUT HIM IS HIS ABSOLUTE COMMITMENT TO THE REGION. HE BELIEVES IN THE CARIBBEAN PERSONALITY, IN THE CARIBBEAN SPIRIT, AND HE SHARES THE CARIBBEAN DREAM. SANDALS IS A TREMEN-DOUSLY SUCCESSFUL HOMEGROWN CARIBBEAN PRODUCT THAT EMBODIES THE REGION AND ALL OF ITS EXPRESSION, COLOR AND CLASS. IT TAKES A FORMIDABLE MIND TO BE ABLE TO CAPTURE SOMETHING LIKE THAT. "

Hon. Dr. Kenny D. Anthony
Prime Minister of St. Lucia

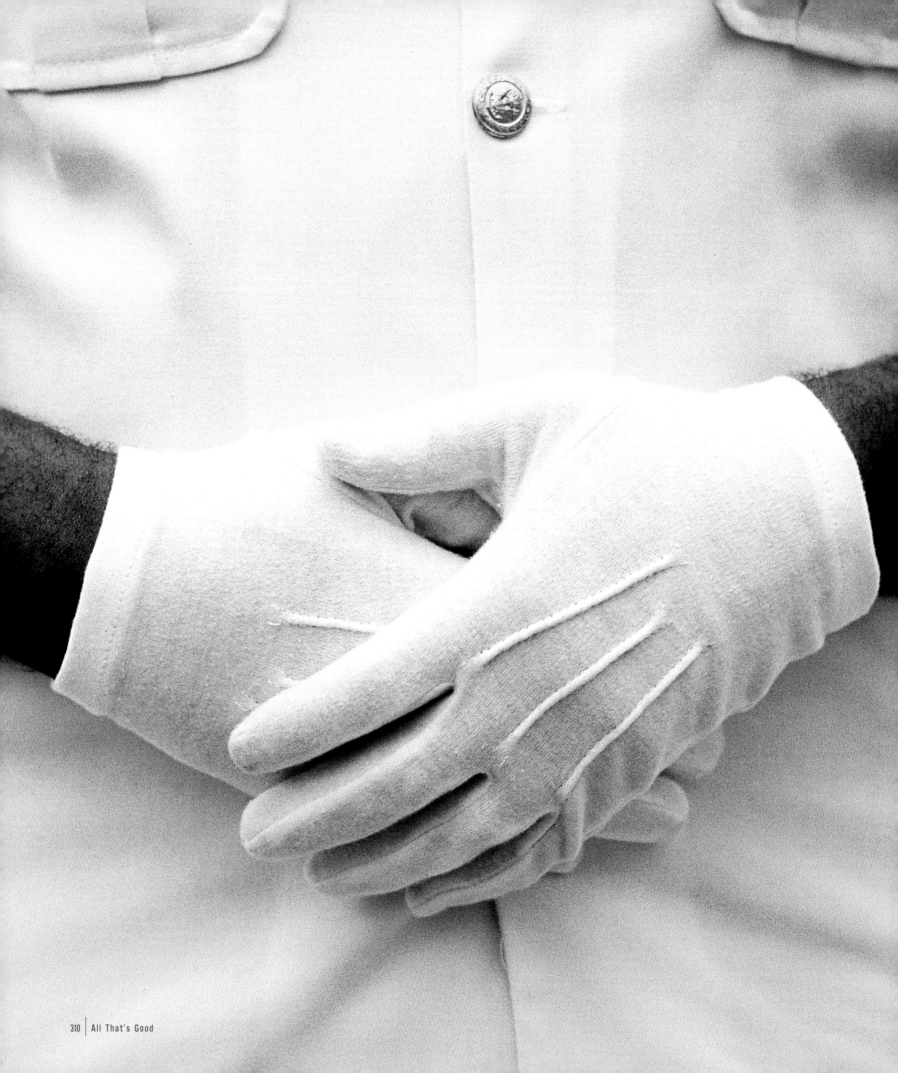

The notion of being first in the marketplace has always been at the forefront of Sandals and at the top of the mind of its innovative chairman, Butch Stewart. In 2005, the bar was raised another notch with the introduction of Butler Service, a first in the all-inclusive industry. Guests vacationing in the highest level suites at Sandals and Beaches resorts now have their every whim catered to by their own personal butler. Taking pride in knowing guests' preferences prior to arrival at the resort, butlers attend to guest needs such as handling private in-suite check-in, packing and unpacking clothes, and even drawing a bubble bath, if the guest so desires.

Nothing compares to having your own personal butler wait on you hand and foot.

"Butler Service takes the suite experience to a whole new level," says Stewart. "Nothing compares to retreating to your own luxurious cliff-top sanctuary, relaxing in your private plunge pool and having your own personal butler wait on you hand and foot."

The butlers at Sandals and Beaches resorts have undergone stringent training and received certification from the London-based Guild of Professional English Butlers. Regarded for its training of individuals worldwide for careers at five-star hotels, royal palaces, embassies and private households, this distinguished guild prides itself on its impeccable butler services.

The resort group has embarked on an exclusive partnership to become the only Caribbean all-inclusive resort member. "We look forward to forging this partnership with Sandals," says Robert Watson, director of training for the Guild of Professional English Butlers. "Our Guild-certified butlers will deliver Caribbean hospitality with an unbelievable English flare for service."

THE BUTLER DID IT
Your martini is delivered promptly. Your warm bath is drawn nightly. Whatever your heart's desire, with Sandals and Beaches Butler Service it's never a problem.

NEW ROMANCE IN OLD JAMAICA

When Butch Stewart purchased property on Jamaica's south coast in 1991, he set out to create a resort that would give tourists a taste of the unspoiled, untamed Jamaica, which had captivated the likes of discoverer Christopher Columbus, swashbuckler Sir Henry Morgan, film legend Errol Flynn and playwright Noel Coward. The new resort is Sandals Whitehouse European Village & Spa.

"This resort is a true gem of Jamaica's south coast," says Butch Stewart. "I am delighted to be able to give vacationers an opportunity to discover the rich culture, history and beauty of this magnificent part of Jamaica."

Set on fifty acres of lushly wooded headland at Parker's Bay in the parish of Westmoreland, Sandals Whitehouse is the first resort development on the unchartered south coast region of Jamaica. With 360 rooms in a collection of "European villages" with Dutch, Italian and French themes, the resort centers on a traditional piazza and is surrounded by tropical greenery and courtyards. The resort also boasts a full-service European spa, seven gourmet restaurants and four swimming pools, one of which is the largest on Jamaica.

Butch Stewart understood that a resort in this undiscovered, glorious part of Jamaica would bring not only a hotel property but also the promise of jobs, training and opportunity to the community. "Tourism means opportunity on Jamaica," says Stewart. "We look forward to a long and mutually rewarding relationship with the incredible people of Westmoreland."

A TASTE OF PARADISE
Top: A peek at the amazing new property. Right: Sandals Whitehouse European Village & Spa lies on the untouched landscape of Jamaica's south coast.

"Sandals Whitehouse is a true gem

of Jamaica's south coast."

drink up

Sandals bartenders created this cocktail in honor of returning guests as a remembrance of their Caribbean stay.

1. Start out by adding 1/2 to 1 inch thick piña colada mix in a glass. This represents the white sand. The coconut in the piña colada brings to mind palm and coconut trees associated with being on a paradise island.

2. Add 3 slices of banana to remind you of shells and tropical fruit.

3. In a blender, mix ice, a shot each of blue Curacao, rum, vodka, and pineapple juice. This creates an image of the turquoise waters of the Caribbean and the pool. Add the mixture slowly so as not to disturb the piña colada at the bottom of the glass.

4. Cut a 1/4 wedge of orange and attach it to the side of the glass. This is symbolic of the warm sun and golden sunsets.

5. Pop in a colorful cocktail umbrella to envision peaceful moments lounging on the beach or by the pool in the colorful hotel environment.

And voilá. The tropical ingredients in this recipe collectively represent the bounty, variety and dining experience associated with being a guest at Sandals and Beaches resorts. Cheers!

HOME AGAIN

With an impressive array of top-quality resorts dotting the Caribbean landscape, it's no wonder that guests keep returning to Sandals and Beaches resorts. In fact, Sandals has among the highest percentage of returning guests in the industry. "We remain dedicated to exceeding guest expectations and providing a level of service that is unsurpassed," says Merrick Fray, managing director for Sandals Resorts International. "Whenever we set out to develop a new program or amenity, first and foremost we consider how it will benefit our guests."

An interesting phenomenon at Sandals is the hard-core cadre of returning guests who consider Sandals their home-away-from-home. "The relationship that our returning guests have with staff is unbelievable," boasts Horace Peterkin, general manager at Sandals Montego Bay. "Many of our returnees have been coming to this resort for decades and they are on a first-name basis with staff. When they arrive, it's like a big family reunion and we take great pride in spoiling them."

For many years, Sandals had an informal returning guest program, complete with weekly "returning guest dinners" and special reunion weeks. The program proved so successful that the company made plans to develop it further.

"When we decided to formalize our returning guest program, the project was assigned to me," says Butch Stewart's son, Bobby Stewart, currently Unique Vacations managing director for the United Kingdom and Europe. The junior Stewart, who has a marketing background, is also an information technology whiz kid and was at the helm of Sandals' IT program for years before moving into corporate marketing. "We have many guests who have returned to Sandals ten, twenty, even fifty times. So we wanted to commemorate those milestones as well as offer incentives to our first- and second-time guests. I spent about two years developing an ideal plan."

The "plan" became known as the Sandals Signature Guest program, which was officially launched in 1999. Today, it is regarded as among the best guest loyalty programs in the industry.

Recalls Bobby Stewart, "We did an initial mailing inviting guests to voluntarily enroll online, and at the same time, we monitored a real-time screen to see registrations as they happened. It was amazing to see the screen go from two members to forty members to three thousand members. Today, we have more than one hundred thousand members enrolled."

Artists on the Isle

The Caribbean's leading art dealer and art auction house, IE Limited represents some of the finest artists from the islands and beyond. IE Limited conducts weekly art auctions at all three Sandals St. Lucia properties. Many stunning contemporary paintings are also accessible through the "caribbeanartandantiques" online gallery and the Rodney Bay, St. Lucia gallery. Here is a sampling of the accomplished artists whose works are available through IE Limited.

P.J. STEWART. A graduate of the Hammersmith College of Art, Stewart creates work that is vibrant and intellectually challenging. A champion for Caribbean artists, she has also commissioned and purchased the work of leading Caribbean artists to enhance many of the Sandals and Beaches resorts.

FLEUR DE ST. LUCIE. The art dealer's most collected artist, de St. Lucie draws much of her inspiration from the Caribbean and from St. Lucia itself. Using water-based paint on silk, de St. Lucie's work is truly representative of the Caribbean's joie de vivre.

ROSS WILSON. With his work represented in London's Tate Gallery and The British Museum, Cambridge's Fogg Museum and Harvard University, and Boston's Museum of Fine Arts, Wilson, who lives and works in Northern Ireland, is considered to be one of the most collected artists of his generation.

LLEWELLYN XAVIER. St. Lucia's most prominent and innovative artist, Xavier creates multimedia work and has been exhibited at some of the world's finest art institutions, including the Metropolitan Museum of Art, the Museum of Modern Art, and the Smithsonian Institution. The artist has been critically reviewed and featured in numerous art books and publications. In 2005, Xavier was awarded the OBE (The Most Excellent Order of the British Empire) by Her Majesty Queen Elizabeth II for his contribution to art. And, the renowned international publisher, Macmillan, has commissioned a biography of the artist.

A FAMILY AFFAIR

While the Sandals team considers its guests as family, many of Stewart's own family members are also part of his company. Three of Butch Stewart's children—Bobby, Jaime and Adam—currently work in managerial positions within the organization. Brian Jardim, Stewart's eldest son, spent several years working with his father before the entrepreneurial spirit struck. He currently owns the Caribbean franchise of the Jimmy Buffet Margaritaville restaurant chain. Stewart's son Jonathan, who passed away in 1990, was an integral part of the team at Sandals' reservations and marketing arm, Unique Vacations.

For Jaime Stewart, going to work for Sandals after graduation in 2000 was innate. "I grew up with Sandals in my veins," says Stewart. "The camaraderie within the Sandals organization, and also within the industry for that matter, is very addicting and comforting. Our work brings people relaxation, love, laughter, and time for themselves and their families. How could I say to my dad, 'I think I would like to be a doctor.' I'd be insane!"

CASUAL TO COCKTAIL
Above: Butch Stewart and Cheryl Hamersmith on their way to St. Lucia. Right: From left to right, Adam Stewart, Jaime Stewart, Butch Stewart and Bobby Stewart are decked out for an elegant evening.

Carisam

Top Stock

Wines, spirits, tobacco, water, soda, perfumes, cosmetics, fine china, and watches are just some of the many provisions that make their way to Sandals and Beaches resorts on a regular basis thanks to Carisam.

This ship chandling company has been distributing goods for consumption to cargo, commercial and cruise ships, as well as to airlines, resorts and hotels, and diplomats, for the past seventeen years. Carisam's roots can be traced back to the 1920s, when the company, known as Samuel Meisel & Co., provided its services to embassies and consultants in the Baltimore and Washington, D.C. area. Today, Carisam services nine hundred diplomatic accounts worldwide; seventeen hundred tankers, freighters and container ships; and more than fifty Caribbean resorts.

Photo: Sandals Resorts International (Royal Plantation)

For more than a decade, Sandals and Beaches Resorts have been honored with almost every major international industry award, including the prestigious AAA Four Diamond Award for superior services, amenities, cuisine and accommodations; the distinguished American Academy of Hospitality Sciences Five Star Diamond Award; *Condé Nast Travelers'* annual Reader's Choice Poll; *Travel and Leisure's* World's Best Award; and various World Travel Awards, among

As Sandals commemorates its remarkable story, the extended family it has helped create celebrates too.

What started as a small air-conditioning business has today grown into the Caribbean's largest private enterprise. The Appliance Traders Group manages some twenty-five businesses—in manufacturing, distribution, newspaper publishing, and tourism. Just as striking to note is the vast number of team members who have been with the group from its early days.

Says one industry admirer of Butch Stewart and the team: "It's incredible that he's been able to engender that sort of loyalty and culture for over twenty, thirty years with this core group. They travel from island to island with him and they have an 'each one, teach one' principle so that the culture flows. He has people like Betty Jo Desnoes, Eleanor Miller, Merrick Fray, David and Brian Roper, Errol Lee, and Larry McDonald who have worked with him for more than two decades, who completely understand him, and who know exactly what he stands for. They've internalized the Sandals concept and passed it along."

As Sandals commemorates its remarkable story, the extended family it has helped create celebrates too. That family includes farmers growing tomatoes on St. Lucia, taxicab drivers shuttling guests to the airport in the Bahamas, travel agents booking trips in Ohio and on Long Island, tour operators selling packages in Ottawa and in the United Kingdom, waiters topping off water glasses on Providenciales, construction workers building a gourmet restaurant on Jamaica's north coast, parents returning home from Beaches with their children, and honeymooners strolling down white-sand beaches at sunset.

Nearly twenty-five years after gambling on a rundown resort, Sandals operates twenty ultra all-inclusive resorts throughout the Caribbean. Today, Butch Stewart, the kid from Ocho Rios, is considered by many to be the unofficial "Prime Minister of the Caribbean." He remains as active as ever and is a staunch and outspoken advocate for the region.

Throughout the challenges, developments, innovations, and accolades, the Sandals team continues to be focused on the singular vision that started it all: giving guests more than they expect.

As Sandals extends its wings to new Caribbean destinations, one thing is certain if the past is any indication of the future—the best is yet to come.

A

Adler Insurance Group
www.adlerinsurance.com
866-662-7200

Agostini Insurance Brokers
(St. Lucia) Limited
aib@agostini-stlucia.com
758-452-4733

Air Canada Vacations
www.aircanadavacations.com
514-876-0700

Air Jamaica
www.airjamaica.com
800-523-5585

Air Jamaica Vacations
www.airjamaicavacations.com
800-LOVEBIRD

American Airlines Vacations
www.aavacations.com
800-321-2121

Anderson Fabrics, Inc.
jande91043@aol.com
304-591-0984

Aqua Sun Video & Photos
aquasun@cwjamaica.com
876-953-3746

Arosa Ltd.
arosa1@cwjamaica.com
876-972-2310

ART Sound Lighting & Video
www.artsoundslv.com
305-666-4202

Associated Manufacturers
www.bushabrowne.com
876-926-6449

A Time to Travel
www.atimetotravelnow.com
800-551-5118

B

Bank of Saint Lucia Ltd.
www.bankofsaintlucia.com
758-456-6000

Blue Mountain Bicycle Tours
www.bmtoursja.com
876-974-7075/7492

Bridal Guide Magazine
www.bridalguide.com
800-472-7744

Brinks St. Lucia Ltd.
brinks@candw.lc
758-452-6342

The Burns House Group of Companies
www.burnshouse.com
242-323-6444

C

Cable & Wireless Jamaica Limited
www.cwjamaica.com
888-225-5295

Cairsea Services
www.cairsea.com
649-946-4205

Captain Mike's Sport Fishing &
Pleasure Cruises
www.captmikes.com
758-452-7044

Caribbean Communications Network
(CCN)
www.ccngroup.com
868-623-1711

Caribbean Metals Limited
cmetals@candw.lc
758-450-2249

Carisam-Samuel Meisel
www.carisamco.com
305-591-3993

C

Carnival Party Cruises
www.carnivalsailing.com
758-452-5586

Chukka Cove Adventure Tours
www.chukkaadventure.com
876-972-2506

Chukka Blue Adventure Tours
www.chukkaadventure.com
876-953-5619

Citibank, Jamaica
www.citibank.com/jamaica
876-926-3270

Classic Custom Vacations
www.classicvacations.com
800-221-3949

Colombian Emeralds International
www.dutyfree.com
877-556-5565

Condé Nast Bridal Group
www.brides.com
www.modernbride.com
212-286-8380

Cool Runnings Spring Water Co. Ltd.
www.coolrunningswater.com
876-940-0581

D

Departures Magazine
www.departures.com
212-642-1940

Dunn's River Falls and Park
www.dunnsriverja.com
876-974-2857/5944/4767

E

Edward Don & Company
www.don.com
954-983-3000

Expedia.com
www.expedia.com
800-EXPEDIA

F

Far Eastern Imports
goodthingsinprovo@hotmail.com
649-941-5055

Ferguson Enterprises
www.ferguson.com
954-726-3951

Flight Centre North America
www.flightcentre.ca
888-WORLD-31

G

Garber Travel
www.garbertravel.com
800-FLY-GARBER

Go Classy Tours, Inc.
www.goclassy.com
800-329-8145

GOGO Worldwide Vacations
www.gogowwv.com
201-934-3500

Green Grotto Caves and Attractions
www.greengrottocaves.com
876-973-2841/3217

Guardian Holdings Limited
www.guardianholdings.com
868-632-5433

Guardsman Limited
caclements.gm@cwjamaica.com
876-928-2246

H

Happy Vacations
www.happy-vacations.com
800-877-4277

Harris Paints (St. Lucia) Ltd.
www.harris.bb
758-450-0727

Heave-Ho Charters
www.heaveho.net
876-974-5367

Hill & Hill
hillandhill@actol.net
268-462-4717

I

IE Limited
www.caribbeanartandantiques.com
758-450-8485

Implementation Ltd.
www.implementationltd.com
876-978-2998

Inter-brand Inc.
www.inter-brandinc.com
954-792-0172

Islands Media
www.islands.com
805-745-7155

J

J. A. Prime Gourmet Foods Inc.
orionja@candw.lc
758-450-2784

J. Wray & Nephew Ltd.
www.appletonrum.com
876-923-6141

Jack Tobin Inc.
jjt8st@aol.com
954-923-5599

JAG Incorporated
jaginc@candw.lc
758-540-4001/4491

Jamaica Broilers Group Limited
ccooke@jabgl.com
876-943-4370

Jamaica Money Market Brokers Ltd.
www.jmmb.com
888-YES-JMMB

Jamaica Tourist Board
www.visitjamaica.com
876-929-9200

Jamaica Tours Ltd.
www.jamaicatoursltd.com
876-953-3700

Jay Stelzer & Associates
www.jaystelzer.com
954-985-0651

Julian's Supermarkets
www.juliansslu.com
758-451-7357

JUTA Tours Ltd.
www.jutatours.com
876-952-0813

K

The Knot
www.theknot.com
1-877-THE-KNOT

L

Larry Kline Wholesale Meats
www.larryklinemeats.com
954-420-0071

Life of Jamaica Limited
www.life-of-ja.com
876-929-8920

Lou Hammond & Associates, Inc.
www.louhammond.com
212-308-8880

M

McNamara & Co.
mcnamara.co@candw.lc
758-452-2662

Mair Russell Grant Thorton
mairrp@cwjamaica.com
876-926-4513

Majestic Tours
www.majesticholidays.com
242-322-2606

Margaritaville
www.margaritavillecaribbean.com
876-979-8041

The Mark Travel Corporation
www.marktravel.com
414-228-7472

Martha Stewart Living Omnimedia
www.marthastewart.com
212-827-8000

MasterCraft International Sales
www.mastercraftinternational.com
361-937-2727

MLT Vacations Inc.
www.worryfreevacations.com
888-225-5658

N
Nassau Paradise Island Promotion Board
www.nassauparadiseisland.com
954-888-5900

New York Magazine
www.newyorkmetro.com
212-508-0700

Northwest Airlines World Vacations
www.nwaworldvacations.com
800-800-1504

P
P/Kaufmann Contract
contractcs@pkaufmanncontract.com
212-292-2200

Patti LaBella Travel
patti.labella@attglobal.net
800-306-2080

Pevonia Botanica Skincare
www.pevonia.com
800-PEVONIA

Pleasant Holidays
www.pleasantholidays.com
800-448-3333

PricewaterhouseCoopers
www.pwc.com/lc
758-452-2511

Protection & Security Ltd.
psl@cwjamaica.com
876-926-6418

R
Rapsody Cruises
876-979-0102

RBTT Financial Holdings Limited
www.rbtt.com
868-625-RBTT

Renwick & Company Ltd.
renwick@candw.lc
758-455-8000

S
Sagicor Financial Group
www.sagicor.com
246-426-1060

Sant Associates Architect
305-662-4297

The Shell Company (W.I.) Limited
www.shell.com
876-928-7301

Signature Vacations
www.signaturevacations.com
416-967-1510

St. Lucia Distillers
sed@sludistillers.com
758-451-4258

St. Lucia Tourist Board
www.stlucia.org
758-452-4094

Steelite International
www.steelite.com
011-44-1782-821000

T
Tortuga Rum Company Ltd.
www.tortugarums.com
345-949-7701

Tourisme Plus
www.tourismeplus.com
514-881-8583

TravelAge West
www.travelagewest.com
310-772-7430

Travel Agent Magazine
www.travelagentcentral.com
212-951-6600

Travel + Leisure Magazine
www.travelandleisure.com
212-382-5600

Travel Impressions, Ltd.
www.travelimpressions.com
631-845-8000

Travelocity.com
www.travelocity.com
888-TRAVELOCITY

Travelweek
www.travelweek.ca
800-727-1429

Travel Weekly
www.travelweekly.com
201-902-1767

Trip Mate Insurance Agency, Inc.
www.tripmate.com
800-888-0432

Ty, Ty, & Ty, Inc.
www.tyrobes.com
305-805-8085

V
Video Ventures Limited
www.videoventureslimited.com
758-456-5000

W
WeddingChannel.com
www.weddingchannel.com
888-750-1550

The pool at Sandals Royal Bahamian Spa Resort & Offshore Island makes a grand statement.

A romantic outdoor wedding at Sandals Antigua Caribbean Village & Spa.

One of the many gourmet dining options at Sandals and Beaches resorts.

The main pool at Sandals Grande St. Lucian Spa & Beach Resort.

The Great House and pool at Sandals Grande Ocho Rios Beach & Villa Resort.

One of the luxury rondoval suites at Sandals Antigua Caribbean Village & Spa.